D1563002

A Guide to
Computerized Project
Scheduling

A Guide to Computerized Project Scheduling

E. William East
Jeffrey G. Kirby

VNR VAN NOSTRAND REINHOLD
———————————— NEW YORK

Printed in the United States of America

Van Nostrand Reinhold
115 Fifth Avenue
New York, New York 10003

Van Nostrand Reinhold International Company Limited
11 New Fetter Lane
London EC4P 4EE, England

Van Nostrand Reinhold
480 La Trobe Street
Melbourne, Victoria 3000, Australia

Nelson Canada
1120 Birchmount Road
Scarborough, Ontario M1K 5G4, Canada

16 15 14 13 12 11 10 9 8 7 6 5 4 3 2 1

Library of Congress Cataloging-in-Publication Data

East, E. William.
    Computerized project scheduling for construction / E. William
East, Jeffrey G. Kirby.
        p. cm.
    ISBN 0-442-23802-9
    1. Construction industry—Management—Data processing.
    2. Scheduling (Management)—Data processing. 3. Microcomputers.
    I. Kirby, Jeffrey G. II. Title.
    TH438.4.E27 1990
    692—dc20   89-48261
                                                        CIP

Foreword

The management of a complicated project requires planning, scheduling, and control of a large number of interdependent activities, and poses a difficult challenge for the project manager. For this reason, project management, and in particular project scheduling, has traditionally been one of the first areas to be computerized. Even though computer-based scheduling systems have been available since the late 1950s, most organizations, especially in construction, refrained from incorporating these tools within their everyday operations, citing as an excuse the high cost of hardware, software, and personnel training. This situation continued until the 1980s, when scheduling software became widely available for personal computers.

The current proliferation of scheduling systems for personal computers is indicated by the fact that more than 100,000 programs were sold in 1986. The widespread use of this technology, however, has also made it clear that there is not enough expertise within the project management profession to efficiently utilize these tools for better project management.

The goal of this book is to help with what is probably the most common project management problem today: how to apply automated project scheduling systems to real-life projects in order to obtain the maximum managerial benefits.

The approach taken here differs from both the traditional textbook exposition of network-based project scheduling and the dry program descriptions found in computer manuals. Scheduling textbooks focus primarily on the analysis of networks and the development of the underlying mathematical models and algorithms. Computer manuals, on the other hand, concentrate on describing the working details of the front-end interface for a particular program, without any explanations as to the philosophy behind the design and use of the software. As such, neither approach addresses the issues of "schedule design," which includes the details of how projects should be broken down into tasks to be assembled together in a computerized framework that can, indeed, be used for effective planning, scheduling, and control of large projects by a living organization with real constraints. This is exactly the void that this book fills.

This book is organized into three parts: Background on Scheduling, Using Computerized Scheduling, and The Future of Scheduling Software. Its organization reflects the needs of four different groups of readers: students, new or infrequent users of scheduling systems, scheduling engineers, and project team members.

For the student, this book provides a basic introduction to "activity on arrow" and "activity on node" scheduling networks, and an overview of the practical capabilities of scheduling software.

For the person that has just purchased scheduling software, or the infrequent schedule user, an introduction to the practical use of microcomputers for scheduling is provided, and step-by-step guidance for the enhanced use of scheduling software to achieve management objectives beyond the simple instructions found in computer manuals is given.

For the scheduling engineer, this book provides a platform for exploring ideas in automated schedule analysis using knowledge-based systems, electronic data exchange, and schedule analysis programming.

Finally, project team members will find the book's numerous illustrations a useful management resource to assist in developing and reviewing scheduling specifications and evaluating conditions leading to claims.

The information contained in this book can be useful for a wide range of projects, from planning a wedding to the development of a space station. Most of the examples are from the construction industry, since schedules are required for most construction contracts. The reader can easily draw an analogy between the construction illustrations and other applications, such as research and development projects, large organizational moves, commercial product development, or even the planning of political campaigns.

The primary strength of this book is that it draws heavily from the extensive experience of the authors in assisting U.S. Army Corps of Engineers personnel with basic scheduling concepts, the selection of microcomputer software, and their efficient utilization in practice to achieve stated management objectives. The authors' unique position and continuous involvement with a wide spectrum of users and scheduling systems has enabled them to develop and present numerous guidelines, ranging from hardware and software selection criteria to supporting organizational structures, information exchange, and effective software utilization.

These guidelines are presented both from the perspective of the contractor as well as the owner, and should prove to be an invaluable aid for designing and supporting similar scheduling systems in other organizations.

Most of the information and advice in this book is quite unique and cannot be found elsewhere. In addition to the numerous guidelines, this book addresses many of the subtleties of scheduling, such as the issues of activity coding and the management and generation of reports for a large number of tasks; the selection of project and resource calendars; the effect of milestones and target dates on project schedules; the pitfalls of default completion and out-of-sequence progress calculations; the development and utilization of scheduling templates; approaches to earned value calculations; float and cost analysis and their effect on claims; the integration of scheduling with other management systems; the application of line-of-balance to resource utilization; the automated preprocessing and postprocessing of large schedules; and the development of standard scheduling data exchange specifications to allow the transfer of information between dissimilar scheduling systems.

The authors should be commended for their dedication in writing a unique and very useful book that will certainly be of great service to the profession.

Photios G. Ioannou
Assistant Professor of Civil Engineering
The University of Michigan
Chairman, Microcomputers in Construction Committee
American Society of Civil Engineers

Acknowledgments

The creation of a book requires a significant effort by more than the listed authors. The development of this book was a process that continued over a five-year period. Initially, the authors received numerous requests for assistance in basic scheduling concepts, along with requests for assistance in the selection and use of scheduling software from a large number of U. S. Army Corps of Engineers personnel. Our response to these requests was to begin to evaluate the relative merits of some of the leading scheduling software products. This lead to more questions on how to use these PC-based scheduling products and consulting on several project schedules. The logical extension of this process was to capture what we had learned into this book.

We would like to recognize the following: Glenn Latta, Larry True, Kristy Tan, Steve LeClerc, Robert Edwards, Justin Smith, Joyce Janiola, Charlie Stapleton, Ron Timmermans, Stanley Green, James Vredenburg, Jim Brown, Steve Hooper, Al Vanderpool, Loran Baxter, Glenn Stinn, and Steven Pinnell, for their support of our efforts and particularly for participating in the development of a software data exchange format that will allow the free exchange of project information between scheduling packages. This format will, in the opinion of the authors, be a significant factor in improving project planning and control. No longer will each player in the project be required to learn another's favorite scheduling package. The significant learning time of new software will be eliminated and the purchase of extra software will not be required. Software developers will benefit also, as a larger spectrum of users will now be able to interface with their products.

The authors would also like to thank Mr. Harvey Levine of The Project Knowledge Group, Mr. William Hinterleitner of Burns and McDonnell, Dr. Brett Gunnick of The University of Missouri at Columbia, Dr. Jesus De La Garza of Virginia Tech, Dr. Terry Ryan of George Mason University, Nei-Jia Yau, Doctoral Candidate, University of Illinois, and Mr. Abhi Basu of Lehrer McGovern Bovis Inc. for their technical comments and support of this text. The mechanics of preparing a draft by two authors, each with their own style and thoughts, was coordinated by Ms. Vida Florez. Her level of commitment to proofing and suggesting improvement is greatly appreciated.

The authors' employer, the U.S. Army Corps of Engineers, Construction Engineering Research Laboratory, also encouraged the development of this book as a means of transferring our accrued knowledge to the project management profession. Authorship is a long and lonely process, and end products would not be developed were it not for the assistance and encouragement of others.

E. William East
Jeffrey J. Kirby

Contents

A Guide to
Computerized Project
Scheduling

Part 1
Background on Scheduling

Chapter 1

The Need for, and Early Development of, Scheduling Tools

THE GANTT CHART

The rapid growth in the availability and power of microcomputers (at a continuously decreasing cost) has made it possible for managers of large projects to effectively analyze the huge amount of information necessary to monitor and control the progress of many interrelated tasks. Previous to the widespread use of the personal computer (PC), the majority of project managers used the analytical scheduling technique developed by Henry L. Gantt.[1] The bar chart, or Gantt chart, provides a visual means for measuring performance against goals. Figure 1.1 is an example of a bar chart.

The tasks of a project are arranged sequentially in the left-hand column, with time-scaled bars reaching from left to right, representing the time necessary to accomplish the task. The current percent progress is posted below or within the bar. At a quick glance, a manager can determine the status of each task within the project and determine whether the percent progress is equivalent to the percent time used. The bar chart highlights slippage and easily identifies what tasks require close supervision.

Consider the process establishing the schedule for a wedding using a Gantt chart. First, those tasks that are necessary would be identified and then listed in a column on the left side of the chart. Next, an

---

[1]Gantt stated that "There is no moral right to decide on the basis of opinion that which can be determined as a matter of fact" *AMA Management Handbook Second Edition*, William K. Fallon, ed. New York: AMACOM (American Management Association), 1983. pp. 2–106.

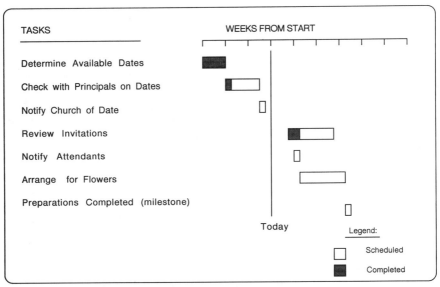

Figure 1.1. Gantt chart for planning a wedding.

estimate of the time to complete each item and when each item starts and finishes would be developed. As time progresses, the estimates of the degree to which each of the tasks are completed are posted to the Gantt chart.

Some tasks have no time associated with them, as they are really decision points or event occurrences. These points are referred to as milestones. Often, the point in time when they must occur is fixed. The task Preparations Completed in Figure 1.1 is an example of a milestone.

Figure 1.1 illustrates that a Gantt chart can be used to identify tasks that are behind schedule. Specifically, Figure 1.1 identifies tasks that are behind schedule. One that is ahead of schedule is also indicated.

The Gantt chart found wide acceptance the early part of the century.[2] For example, the construction time for cargo ships during

---

[2]*Handbook of Industrial Engineering*, Gavriel Salvendy, ed. New York: John Wiley and Sons, 1982. p. 11.2.13.

World War I was reduced significantly by using the Gantt chart. This tool is still widely used today.

The Gantt chart, although simple to understand and formulate, becomes ineffective for projects that require a large number of tasks that are interrelated.[3] The Gantt chart in Figure 1.1 does not show that delaying checking with principals will delay other activities, such as choice of church date, and arranging for flowers.

CPM DEVELOPMENT

It was not until the 1950s that separate independent development efforts were undertaken by both the Dupont Corporation and the U.S. Navy to produce an improved project management tool for complex projects.[4]

The Dupont Corporation, in conjunction with the Remington Rand Corporation, wanted to develop a better system to schedule their refinery modernization projects. The goal was to minimize the down time of the refinery while it was undergoing an upgrade. This goal had to be balanced against the cost of expediting the construction process. Their combined efforts produced the Critical Path Method (CPM[5]). Dupont found that this approach took about half as much time as other scheduling methods and produced significant cost savings on each refinery project.

In a parallel activity, the U.S. Navy and Lockheed Company developed the Program Evaluation and Review Technique (PERT) to assist with the management of the development of the Polaris Program. PERT, although similar to CPM, incorporated statistical estimates of time within the schedule. Three time estimates are required with PERT; most likely, pessimistic, and optimistic. PERT is credited with saving 18 months in the development of the Polaris.

Multiple time estimates required for PERT are cumbersome to use and estimates produced are more difficult to manage, since

---

[3]*Handbook of Construction Management and Organization, Second Edition*, Joseph P. Frein, ed. New York: Van Nostrand Reinhold, 1980. p. 443.
[4]*Project Management with CPM and Pert, Second Edition*, Joseph J. Moder and Cecil R. Phillips. New York: Van Nostrand Reinhold, 1970. pp. 5–7.
[5]In this book, CPM will refer to critical path scheduling systems in a general sense—not a particular class of software programs or a particular vendor product.

project durations can be shown to be correct only 50 percent of the time.[6] Due to this difficulty, PERT is not as widely used as CPM.

In the 1950s, these two efforts were the beginning of the use of CPM to manage schedules for large projects. The spread of this technology throughout the construction industry was slow for several reasons. First, the technology was not widely known. Second, it was some years until it was regularly taught in university courses. Perhaps most important, the application of CPM to a large-scale project required access to a large mainframe computer.

CPM utilization experienced a slow growth in the construction industry in the 1960s, as the larger firms began to purchase mainframe computers for applications other than accounting. The successful introduction of what were then moderately priced high-power minicomputers in the 1970s accelerated the use of CPM in the construction industry. However, the full potential of this valuable tool was still hampered, because almost all of the then-current machines were in the company's home office, and the direct project manager interface with the machine was via third party keypunch operators, who input data and report requests via batch operations. This approach introduced substantial data entry errors and a long time duration between data submittal and the receipt of output reports. The project manager would receive a CPM and various reports anywhere from 2 to 4 weeks after update submission. Since these were not "real-time" or even "near-time" reports, their usefulness was limited.

MICROCOMPUTER-BASED CPM

Until the microcomputer industry matured to the point of the creation of machines containing significant computational power (AT[7] class of computers), the use of CPM was still limited to large construction firms that had ready access to mainframe machines or large minicomputers and scheduling consultants. Although a signifi-

---

[6]*Handbook of Construction*, p. 451.
[7]AT refers to the IBM-introduced Advanced Technology PC in 1986, which included the 80286 full 16-bit processor. This machine represented a significant step forward for PCs in terms of performance.

cant number of software packages were available for microcomputers in the early 1980s, it was not until 1986, when the AT class of personal computers (PC AT) appeared in large numbers, that automated scheduling for large projects became cost effective for a large number of applications within construction and other industries. By 1987, there were over two hundred PC-based scheduling packages from which to choose.[8]

With an investment of approximately $5,000, a project manager can now purchase a PC and compatible CPM software. Before covering the typical features of scheduling software, and how to effectively manage with CPM, the concept of what CPM is and how to develop a CPM will be reviewed in Chapter 2.

---

[8]*Buyers guide to Project Management Software*, Kenneth M. Stepman, ed. Milwaukee, WI: New Issues Inc., 1987.

Chapter 2

Basic Scheduling Techniques

INTRODUCTION

This chapter will present a brief introduction to how a network is created and how the critical path is identified. This information will serve as a basis for later chapters, which identify the means to analyze data from a CPM. Beginning scheduling students will find an introduction to the two types of network presentations: The Arrow Diagram Method (ADM) and the Precedence Diagram Method (PDM). Differences between the two methods are identified. Scheduling practitioners may desire to proceed to Chapter 3.

THE CRITICAL PATH METHOD (CPM)

The CPM method was developed to assist managers of large projects in the tracking of all of the tasks that have to be accomplished. The approach taken is to divide a complex project into manageable components, and then estimate the time required for each component to be completed.

The real power of CPM is in its handling of the interrelationships of all of these tasks. As discussed in Chapter 1, the Gantt chart does not indicate interrelationships. If all tasks are sequential and independent, then a Gantt chart is adequate. For those projects with a large number of interrelated tasks, a CPM is the correct scheduling approach.

The importance of CPM is that it does considerably more than just identify task interrelationships. CPM can also identify the controlling path through these tasks. That is to say, it can identify exactly which of a project's tasks controls the completion date of the project. The critical path is the *longest* path through the network. The longest path has no extra, or float time, included in any of its activities. Each activity must be completed on schedule if the project is to be completed on time. This provides a project manager with a powerful tool for effective management. A CPM will narrow the focus of attention from all tasks to those on the critical path. If those tasks critical to successful completion of the project are on schedule, then the manager can be confident that the entire project is on schedule.

The tracking of a CPM alone does not guarantee a successful project, as it is but one of a host of tools and techniques that contribute to success. The critical path does not remain fixed during a project's lifetime, so constant attention to the schedule is required. CPM software package does the tedious calculations for you, as well as identifying the critical path for the project manager. Freed from this computational chore, the project manager can focus his or her efforts into managing those tasks on, or those close to being on, the critical path.

There are two current varieties of CPM. These are commonly referred to as the Arrow Diagram Method (ADM) and the Precedence Diagram Method (PDM). Each method adds together the time needed for all tasks to complete the project, and determines the critical path through the network. The diagrammatic presentations are different for each method. Both methods have their own strengths and weaknesses.

In order to demonstrate ADM and PDM, a simple construction project will be examined. In this simple construction project, the contractor is required to install two new short sections of pipe, which will connect to an existing pipe system. A manhole connects these two new pipe sections. Nearby electrical lines will also need to be relocated because of the project. Figure 2.1 provides a plan view of the project.

When thinking about planning this small project, three questions should be asked, "What small tasks have to be completed to finish the project?," "Which of these tasks should be done first?," and "How long will it take to finish each task?" Scheduling a project requires that these questions be answered.

There are several ways to accomplish this sample project. One is to relocate the electrical line, excavate the entire pipe trench, install both lengths of pipe, install the manhole, backfill the entire pipe trench, and sod the area that was torn up by the construction. If

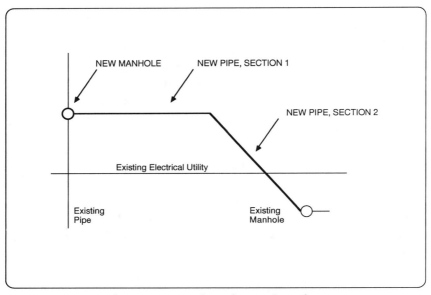

Figure 2.1. Plan view of example project.

time was short and more than one group of workers were available, installing the pipe and beginning backfilling as soon as possible might be attempted.

To keep track of a project, all tasks should be identified and listed. In addition, the relationships between tasks or activities should also be identified.[1] Identifying the list of tasks and how they could follow one another is exactly what is required for CPM. Table 2.1 provides a format that is quite useful in the creation of a schedule. First, all of the activities that need to be done are listed in the center column, *Activity Description*. Next, the activities are sequentially numbered in the left-hand column. Finally, the number of the activity that should follow a given activity is written in the right-hand column. For example, the activity "Install Pipe Section One" has an activity number of 4 and is followed by activity 5, "Backfill Section One," and activity 6, "Install Pipe Section Two."

---

[1]Activity and task will be used interchangeably from now on.

Table 2.1. Activities for a sample project.

ACTIVITY NUMBER	ACTIVITY DESCRIPTION	FOLLOWING ACTIVITIES	DURATION
1	Start Job	2, 3	1
2	Relocate Electric	10	6
3	Excavate	4	5
4	Install Pipe Section One	5, 6	10
5	Backfill Section One	7	5
6	Install Pipe Section Two	7, 8	12
7	Backfill Section Two	9	8
8	Test Pipe Sections	9, 10	3
9	Grade and Sod	12	7
10	Install Manhole	11	3
11	Test Relocated Electric	11	2
12	Final Inspection	none	1

CPM scheduling takes this information and develops two types of pictures that allow a person to quickly understand the flow of work. The Arrow Diagram Method (ADM) represents each activity on an arrow. The arrow indicates the flow of work. It begins at the feather end of the arrow and ends at the point. The feather end, or start, is referred to as the "i" node, and the point end, the "j" node. Thus, the activity is often referred to in terms of its numeric "i,j" notation.

The other presentation form is the Precedence Diagram Method (PDM). In this form, activities are presented on the node and the relationships are indicated by lines. Before constructing a network for the sample project, the concepts of developing an ADM-based network will first be reviewed, and a brief discussion of ADM will be presented. Later, the PDM analog will be presented.

The order of presentation in this book follows the development sequence — ADM appeared first, followed by PDM. The order does not indicate the authors' preferences for ADM and PDM, which will be discussed later in the book.

ARROW DIAGRAM METHOD (ADM)

Before displaying an ADM picture of the information in Table 2.1, the basics of the ADM will be discussed.

There are five basic rules for an ADM listed in the following paragraphs.

Rule 1. An arrow represents a unique activity that occurs between each node. That is to say, two separate activities cannot be drawn between the same two nodes or have the same i,j designation. The solution to this situation is to introduce another activity (a dummy) to make the other parallel path unique (Fig. 2.2).

Rule 2. All activities that end at a node must be completed before an activity can start from that node. In other words, all preceding activities must be completed before any successor activities can start (Fig. 2.3).

Rule 3. All activities leaving a node must be dependent upon the completion of activities entering the node. If a relationship exists, but the preceding activities need not be completed prior to starting, then dummies should be introduced to indicate that there is a relationship but not a dependency (Fig. 2.4).

Rule 4. All projects should have a single starting and ending point (Fig. 2.5).

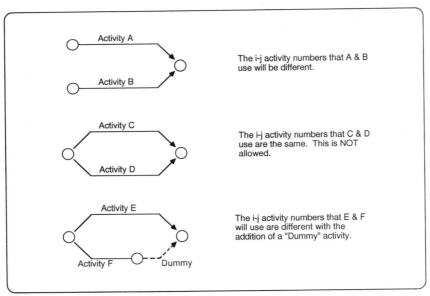

Figure 2.2. Paths between nodes must be unique.

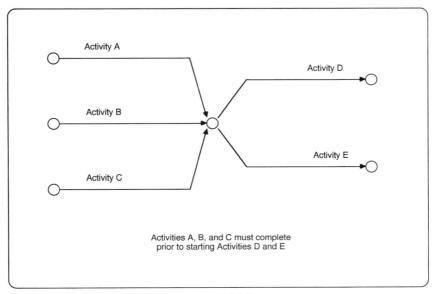

Figure 2.3. All preceding activities must be complete.

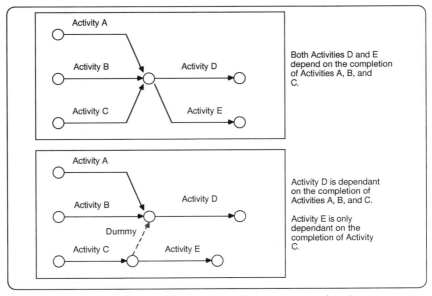

Figure 2.4. Leaving dates are dependent upon entering dates.

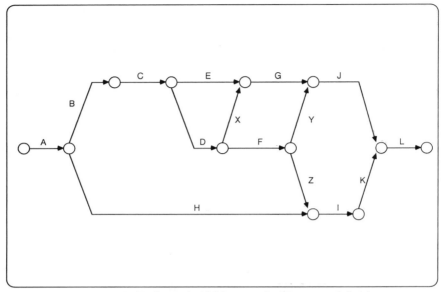

Figure 2.5. Projects should have a single start and finish.

Rule 5. No activity, or its subsequent activities, can be its predecessor. This rule means that no loops are allowed in the network logic (Fig. 2.6).

DEVELOPMENT OF AN ACTIVITY ON AN ARROW (ADM) DIAGRAM

An ADM for the sample project can be constructed using the five rules stated above, and the information contained in Table 2.1. First, a single starting point is necessary (Rule 4). For convenience, the nodes of the example project will be numbered by multiples of five. This option will allow us (at a later date) to add, if necessary, additional activities with a "close" number. From node 10 on Figure 2.7, the end of "Start Job," Table 2.1 indicates two successor activities: activity number 2 (10,45), which is "Relocate Electric," and activity 3 (10,15), "Excavate." Activities 4, 5, and 6 from Table 2.1 are added to complete Figure 2.7.

Notice that, from Table 2.1, activity 6, "Install Pipe Section Two," has two successors: activity 7, "Backfill Section Two," and

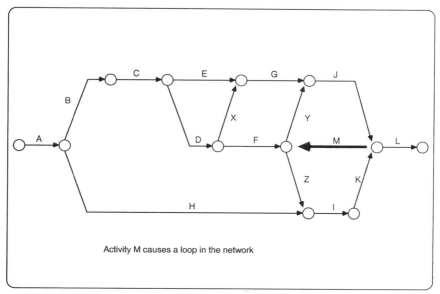

Activity M causes a loop in the network

Figure 2.6. Loops are not allowed.

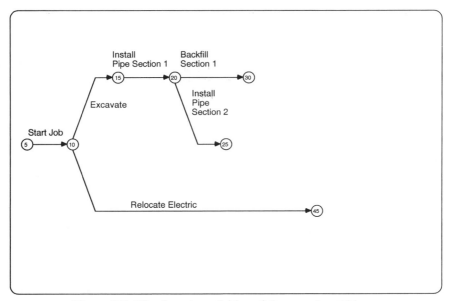

Figure 2.7. The first six activities of the sample problem.

activity 8, "Test Pipe Sections." The first relationship is simply a logical link. After the completion of "Install Pipe Section Two," "Backfill Section Two" can commence. Since no time or resources are necessary to accomplish this activity, it is referred to as a logical dummy, i,j (25,30) and is indicated by a dashed arrow. Activity 8 is indicated in the normal manner. These additions to Figure 2.7 are shown in Figure 2.8.

In completing the ADM diagram, the error shown in Figure 2.9 might be made. From Table 2.1, activity 8, "Test Pipe Sections," "Install Manhole" and "Grade and Sod" are indicated as successors. The network, as drawn in Figure 2.9, does indicate that relationship, but it also incorrectly implies that grading and sodding and the installation of the manhole can not begin until the pipe testing is completed (Rule 3).

The complete, correctly drawn sample problem is obtained by the addition of two additional logical dummies, to indicate only the logical dependencies of the grading and sodding (activity 9) and installation of the manhole (activity 10) with the completion of the testing of the pipe sections (activity 8). See Figure 2.10.

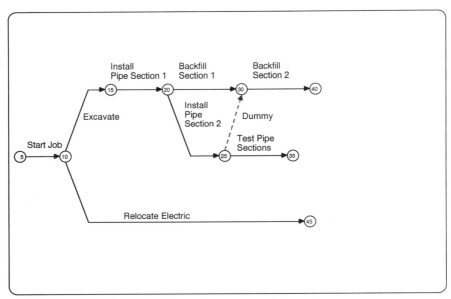

Figure 2.8. The first eight activities of the sample network.

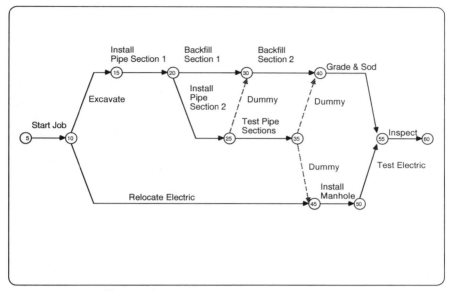

Figure 2.9. Incorrect complete sample project.

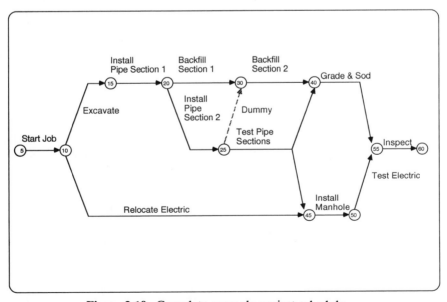

Figure 2.10. Complete example project schedule.

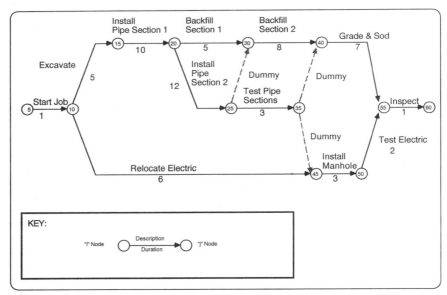

Figure 2.11. Example project schedule, with durations.

The next step in developing an ADM diagram is the addition of the durations from Table 2.1. Activity durations, in terms of work days to complete, are normally listed below the arrow, as shown in Figure 2.11.

DEFINITION OF TERMS

Mathematical analysis of an ADM or PDM network consists of finding the early start and finish dates, late start and finish dates, and the float associated with each activity. The float is of major interest to the project manager.

1. *Early Start Date.* The Early Start (ES) date of an activity is the earliest date that all required previous activities can have been completed (Rule 2), so that this activity can commence.

2. *Late Start Date.* The Late Start (LS) date is the latest date that this activity can begin and not have a negative impact on the project completion date. This assumes that the duration estimate is good and that required resources are available.

3. *Early Finish Date.* The Early Finish (EF) date is the earliest

date that an activity can be completed. The EF is equal to the ES plus the duration of the activity.

4. *Late Finish Date.* The Late Finish (LF) date is the latest date that an activity can be completed and not have a negative impact on the project completion date. Mathematically, the LF equals the LS plus the duration of the activity.

5. *Total Float.*[2] The total float is the difference between the LS and the ES (or the LF and EF) of that activity. It is a measure of the total time, beyond the activity duration, that is available before this activity becomes critical (i.e., negatively impacts the completion time of the entire project). Since the ES and EF are, in fact, determined by all activities in a path, all activities in a particular path will normally have the same float. This float represents the total time window available after the ES for any activity within this path to begin and still not have a negative impact on the project completion date. That is to say, as long as an activity begins during the time frame identified between its ES and LS, no project slippage will occur. Mathematically, the activity float equals the EF minus the ES, or the LF minus the LS.

CALCULATION OF THE EARLY START/FINISH

An understanding of how the LS and ES dates are calculated is important. These dates will be derived for the sample problem. Hand calculations are seldom performed now, since numerous CPM software programs for personal computers exist. However, it is important to know how to do the calculations by hand, since it provides a good understanding of how the process works.

Of key interest to the project manager is the question "how soon can each activity be started?" The Early Start for each activity is identified by the following reasoning process. Using the project start date, begin at the first activity and then follow through the chain of activities to determine when is the earliest date that each of the

---

[2]Many scheduling texts refer to activity free float, which is the difference between the earliest start time of a successor activity and the earliest finish time of the activity. Free float is the amount of time an activity can be delayed without impacting the earliest start of following activities. Since the practical use of this concept is limited, and it is not typically used by automated scheduling packages, it will not be discussed further.

activities can begin. The ES of any activity is the EF of its predecessor. The EF of a predecessor is its ES plus its duration.

Calculation of the ES for the ADM, which is also sometime referred to as the *forward pass*, progresses from the start towards the finish. In the sample problem, the starting point (node 5) is assigned an early start time of 0. Thus the ES of activity (5,10) is 0. The ES of those activities starting from node 10 is determined by calculating the EF of activity (5,10), which starts from node 5. In this case, it is 0 plus 1, which equals 1, and is the ES for those activities beginning at node 10. The calculated ES date for those activities starting from the node is shown in a box above the node. Similarly, the ES for activities beginning at nodes 15, 20, 25, and 35 are calculated and presented in Figure 2.12.

When two or more activities terminate at the same node, the path to that node that yields the latest EF will be the ES for all activities leaving that node. The basis for this is Rule 2, all preceding activities must be completed prior to beginning an activity. Thus, the ES for all activities is determined by selecting the latest preceding EF. This is accomplished by adding the duration to each preceding ES and

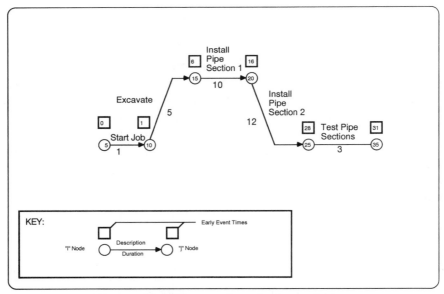

Figure 2.12. Early start times for first activities.

comparing the results. A mnemonic device for remembering this rule is "maximize the entering values." This rule must be applied to activities (30,40), (40,55), (45,50), and (55,60). For activity (30,40), the ES for the route from node 20 is 16 plus 5, or 21. The second route to node 30, via activities (20,25) and (25,30), provides an ES of 28 (16 plus 12). Note that this is the same ES as for activity (25,30), which starts at node 25, since this activity is a logical dummy, and has no duration. Using the "maximize the entering values" rule, we find that the ES for activity (30,40), departing node 30, is 28. Similarly, the ES for (40,55) is equal to 36, that for (45,50) is equal to 31, and that for (55,60) is equal to 43. Note that the ES for node 60 corresponds to the earliest time that the project can be completed, which is 44 days after starting. These values are indicated in Figure 2.13.

CALCULATION OF THE LATE START/FINISH

The LS and LF for each activity is calculated in a similar manner, but the process begins at the end and works back toward the begin-

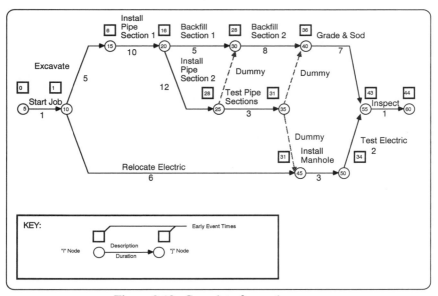

Figure 2.13. Complete forward pass.

ning. Recall that the ES determines the earliest time that a project can be completed. This information is used to determine "how late can activities be initiated and still not negatively impact the desired (early) finish date?" Since we start with the desired finish date, which is the EF date, we must work backwards through the chain of activities to identify the latest possible start dates that will not negatively impact the completion date.

The procedure, sometimes referred to as the *backward pass*, is as follows: the late start of an activity is equal to the late finish of its successor minus its duration. In the example, the LF of activity (55,60) is set equal to the EF, or 44, since this is the starting point for our calculations. The LS is normally indicated in a triangle below the node. The LS of (55,60) is 44 minus 1, or 43. Applying this principle, the LS for node (50,55) is equal to 41, that for (45,50) is equal to 38, that for (40,55) is equal to 36, and that for (30,40) is equal to 28. See Figure 2.14.

Nodes 35, 20, and 10 can be reached by more than one route during the calculation of the LS. The mnemonic for the rule here is the converse of that for the forward pass: "minimize the values

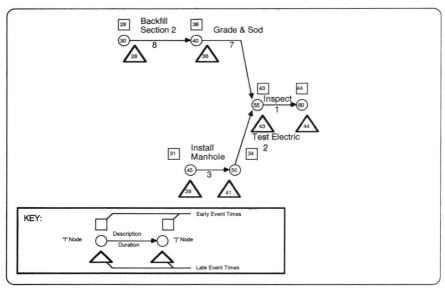

Figure 2.14. Partial backward pass.

leaving" the node. The rationale is again based upon Rule 2. The LS is the latest date for an activity to begin and still allow for completion of the project on time with certainty. If a node has two outbound arrows, the lowest (numerically) value is selected during the calculation of the LS. This earlier date is the last date that all activities can be started and completed from that node without the project being delayed. In the example, node 35 can be reached via node 40 (the LS is equal to 36 minus 0, or 36) or via node 45 (38 minus 0, or 38). Applying the "minimize the values leaving" rule will cause the selection of 36 as the correct LS for (35,40) and (35,45). Continuing to apply the rule will determine the LS for (20,30) and (20,25) to be 16, and that for (5,10) as 1. These values are presented in Figure 2.15.

The critical path through the network is where the ES is equal to the LS. Since no float exists, each task is on what is referred to as the critical path. This is the longest path through the network and requires that all activities must be completed on time for the project to be finished on time. No float, or extra time, exists on the critical path, and the difference between EF minus ES, or LF minus LS, will

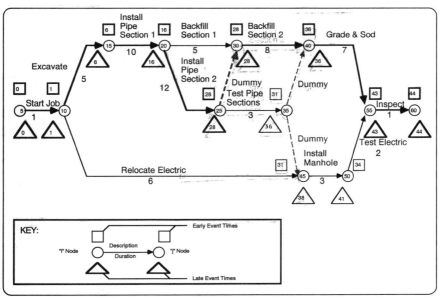

Figure 2.15. Forward and backward pass with critical path.

equal the duration for that activity. For our example: the critical
path is (5,10), (10,15), (15,20), (20,25), (25,30), (30,40), (40,55), and
(55,60). This path is darkened in Figure 2.15.

DIFFERENCES BETWEEN ADM AND PDM

The ADM (or arrow diagramming) was the first, of the two methods
discussed in this chapter, to be used to schedule construction projects. The power of the ADM is in its intuitive simplicity. It is very
easy, even for a person with little scheduling experience, to grasp
that each task to be performed is an arrow and that each subsequent
arrow represents the next activity to be completed. An arrow diagram that specifically relates the number of days or weeks to the
length of an arrow is called a "time-scaled" arrow diagram. Even if
the arrow diagram is not scaled, as in Figure 2.15, the concept of a
relative time-line is very clear. This ease of understanding is the
biggest selling point of the ADM.

The difficulty with the ADM is that an activity typically starts and
stops at the beginning and end of other activities. An activity that
must be completed prior to the next activity starting is referred to as
having a finish-to-start relationship. This is clearly shown in Figure
2.15 as "Start Job" (5,10), which has a finish-to-start relationship
with "Excavate" (10,15) and "Relocate Electric" (10,45).

Construction is generally not as simple as this. For example, once
a concrete wall is poured, it begins to cure. Before the wall is
completely cured, the forms may be stripped and placed in another
location. The activities "Place and Cure Concrete," and "Strip
Forms," are related by what is called a "start-to-start" relationship
with a time lag. This means that, several days after the start of the
activity "Place and Cure Concrete," the activity "Strip Forms" may
start.

To represent the start-to-start type of construction sequence with
ADM is quite cumbersome, as the initial activity, "Place and Cure
Concrete," must be divided into two serial activities so that "Strip
Forms" can be connected at their joining point. Exactly this prob-
lem occurred with the sample problem, with the *install pipe* and
backfill activities. The install pipe activity was divided into two
components, "Install Pipe Section One" and "Install Pipe Section
Two." At the completion of "Install Pipe Section One," the activity

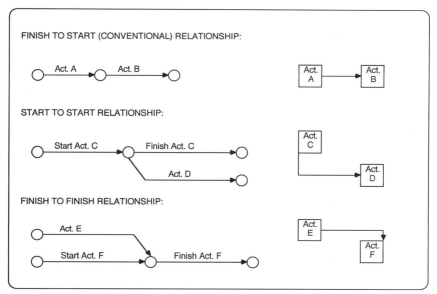

Figure 2.16. Arrow and precedence comparison.

"Backfill Section One" was begun. Figure 2.16 demonstrates how PDM can present these relationships in a better visual form. The node or box represents the activity, and the arrows simply represent the relationships.

To represent the ADM example pipe project in Figure 2.15, twelve activities and three dummy activities were required. These "dummy" activities are necessary to reflect the logical relationships between, first, the completion of the second section of pipe (20,25) and the start of the second backfill operation (30,40), and second, the completion of pipe testing (25,35), the completion of the backfill (30,40), and beginning the installation of the manhole (45,50). A direct transfer of Figure 2.15 into a PDM diagram (Figure 2.17) presents a much simpler picture of the work required, with only 12 activities (no dummies are required).

The PDM is able to handle more complex activity relationships, such as start-to-start and finish-to-finish, without having to introduce dummies. To use PDM, ADM schedulers must change their perceptions of how time is represented on an activity. Although the ADM and PDM diagrams look similar, because of the relationships

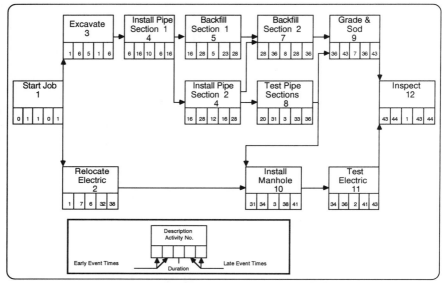

Figure 2.17. Example project translated into PDM.

between the activities, the relationship lines between PDM activities have no time associated with them, as they serve to indicate relationships only.

The advantage of presenting the example pipe project in PDM is shown in Figure 2.17. Notice that no dummy activities are necessary in the PDM network to reflect the logical relationships between activities. In fact, several activities could have even been combined. Split activities, such as "Install Pipe Section One" and "Install Pipe Section Two," or "Backfill Section One" and "Backfill Section Two," could be combined into one activity. To take into account the delay between starting backfill after starting piping, the scheduler would create a backfill activity that starts seventeen days after the start of the piping operations. The effect of introducing the concept of a "lag" is demonstrated in Figure 2.18. Notice that this figure is even less complicated, since only 10 activities are now necessary to represent the sample project. Notice how Figure 2.18 is much easier to follow than Figure 2.15. The location of date notations are located within the box. The calculation of the forward and backward passes are accomplished in the same manner as for ADM.

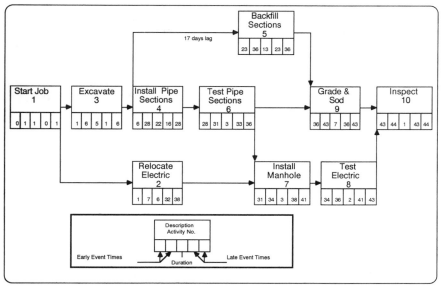

Figure 2.18. Simplified example project using lags.

On large projects, PDM can produce a network diagram that is considerably less complicated than an ADM approach. Since PDM reduces the number of activities required to depict the project, it also reduces the calculations necessary to accomplish the forward and backward passes. In the sample problem, PDM was able to present the project while using one-third less activities. On a complicated project involving thousands of activities, the benefits of a PDM approach will be significant.

Debates are often heated as to whether ADM or PDM is the better scheduling approach. Both models may contain the exact same information. At the start of this chapter, we noted that there are three elements of a network: (1) activity descriptions, (2) activity relationships, (3) and activity durations. Both models contain this information. Since the main purpose of scheduling is to facilitate the agreement of the project management team on a plan of action, then the best strategy is to select the model that all parties best understand.

The benefits of using either method are similar, but different. ADM can model the flow of work, especially if a time-scaled diagram is required. The need to use dummies to represent the "correct" logic can be confusing. ADM was developed first, and a considerable number of schedulers have fully mastered this approach. PDM is better at representing complex or repetitive construction projects, because it is simpler to represent the interrelationships of overlapping tasks. For practical reasons, it is prudent for a scheduler to know both methods.

Part 2

Using Computerized Scheduling

Chapter 3

Basic Microcomputer Scheduling Techniques

INTRODUCTION

After the basics of scheduling, presented in Chapter 2, have been mastered, the next step is to begin to use one or more of the available personal computer-based scheduling systems. The scheduling systems will not only automatically and quickly perform forward and backward passes, but will also provide the following capabilities: a comparison of the current schedule with the baseline plan, evaluation of the results of what-if scenarios, quick and efficient retrieval of specific reports on any particular activity or related group of activities, and the automatic calculations of cost and resource requirements.

This chapter will introduce the procedure for entering a project into a PC-based scheduling system, and also examine the correct method for scheduling the project. Both the novice and the seasoned practitioner will benefit from the recommendations on how to effectively code a project for data entry. The following chapters will demonstrate effectively structuring information retrievals in order to maximize the usefulness of a CPM to manage a project.

In order to use one of the PC scheduling packages, the same information that would be manually used to schedule the project will need to be input into the computer. Almost all scheduling systems require that three basic operations be completed before they can calculate a forward and backward pass. These operations are: creating a project, entering activity data, and establishing the work calendar. Commercial scheduling systems also allow updating of the schedule data to reflect project progress.

This chapter provides a basic overview of the three input steps that most software packages require prior to their being able to calculate a schedule. Once the program has been properly installed on the hard disk of the PC, the following information should be used in conjunction with the program's user manual. Since these generic features are required for almost all scheduling systems, the information in this chapter should enable the use of almost any scheduling system.

CREATING A PROJECT

The first option in a scheduling program that should be selected is to create a new project: this is generally called "Add a New Project." This option will, typically, appear after the program is started and the first opening "menu," or list of choices, is presented. Typically, the program will prompt the user to select the letter or number corresponding to "Add a New Project."

Standard PC menus can easily be recognized, as they are presented as a list, and are usually positioned in the middle of the computer screen. Figures 3.1 and 3.2 are examples of the opening menus used in the Primavera and PlanTRAC scheduling systems.

```
                    PRIMAVERA UTILITIES
                    ~~~~~~~~~~~~~~~~~~~~

        The following projects are contained in the directory:

                         BASE   CAR4

                SELECT an existing project.......1
                LIST project names and titles....2
                ADD a new project................3
                DELETE a project.................4
                DUPLICATE and rename project.....5
                MERGE several projects...........6
                MAINTAIN target plans............7
                BACKUP one or more projects......8
                RESTORE one or more projects.....9
                SUMMARIZE projects into master...0

                   PRIMAVISION.....................P
                   CONFIGURE PRIMAVERA.............C
                   EXIT...........................X

                Press selection █
```

Figure 3.1. Primavera Utilities initial menu. (Primavera Project Planner, Version 3.2. *Courtesy of Primavera Systems, Inc.*)

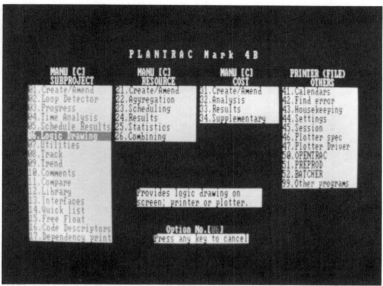

Figure 3.2. PlanTRAC initial menu. (PlanTRAC 4B. *Courtesy of Computerline, Inc.*)

Top or bottom line menus are categorized by listing their options on either the top two or bottom two lines of the computer screen. The user selects an option by either pressing a designated letter of the option, often capitalized and highlighted, or by moving a high-lighted bar with the arrow keys over the option and pressing the "Enter" (or the "Return") key. If the selection requires a choice of other menus, these will often be shown as the highlighted bar passes through each option.

The pull-down menu is the next type of interface used in some scheduling software. The pull-down menu is a form of the top or bottom line menu, but it is more graphic and can be used with a mouse. The user selects the action to be performed in two steps. The first step is to move a highlighted bar, via the arrow keys or a mouse to the top line, where the general menu is typically located. Once in place, another menu "pulls-down" and appears. The highlighted bar is then moved on top of the desired menu choice. Figures 3.3 and 3.4 are examples of pull-down menus from the ViewPoint and Open Plan systems.

Once you have pressed the key corresponding to your selection to

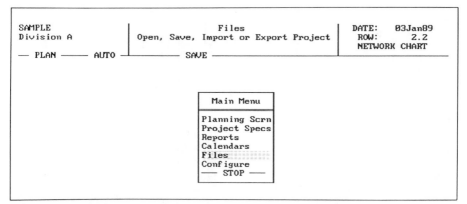

Figure 3.3. ViewPoint pull-down menu. (ViewPoint, Version 3.1. *Courtesy of Computer Aided Management, Inc.*)

add a new project, several pieces of information will be required on a data entry form. Figure 3.5 shows a project data entry screen for the PMS-II system. Each piece of data required for entry is shown next to a highlighted or underlined space. Required data includes the project number, title, the contractor's name, the project start

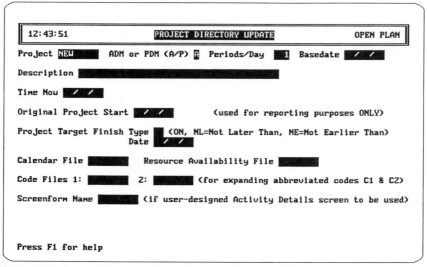

Figure 3.4. Open Plan project directory update pull-down menu. (Open Plan, Version 3.2. *Courtesy of Welcom Software Technology*)

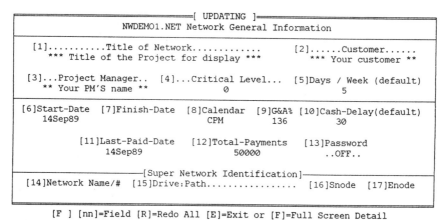

```
==============================[ UPDATING ]==============================
                 NWDEMO1.NET Network General Information

 [1]..........Title of Network............        [2]......Customer......
    *** Title of the Project for display ***         *** Your customer **

 [3]...Project Manager..  [4]...Critical Level...  [5]Days / Week (default)
    ** Your PM'S name **              0                      5

 [6]Start-Date  [7]Finish-Date  [8]Calendar  [9]G&A% [10]Cash-Delay(default)
    14Sep89                         CPM          136          30

           [11]Last-Paid-Date    [12]Total-Payments    [13]Password
               14Sep89               50000                ..OFF..

 ─────────────────────[Super Network Identification]────────────────────
 [14]Network Name/#  [15]Drive:Path.................  [16]Snode  [17]Enode
```

```
     [F ] [nn]=Field [R]=Redo All [E]=Exit or [F]=Full Screen Detail
```

Figure 3.5. PMS-II network general information data screen. (PMS-II, Version 9.0. *Courtesy of North America Mica, Inc.*)

date, ADM or PDM network, network model specifications, the duration and start of the work week, work calendars and nonwork holidays, and project (activity code) libraries. Often, scheduling software will use predetermined, or default, values for these items, if you do not specify values. To eliminate incorrect assumptions, you should always specify this information. Each of these items will be discussed in this chapter. Figure 3.6 shows a PMS80 project data screen.

The "create project" information must clearly identify what construction project is being scheduled. This is not an easy process if multiple projects are to be analyzed and the scheduling software only allows the user to create and select projects based on a four-character project number, which is typical of several systems. For example, if the last four digits of the U.S. Army Corps of Engineers contract number DACA-89-C-0315 were utilized (0315), this type of contract identification number may not be sufficient on projects that span several years. In this example, the contract number in fiscal year 1989 has a number of the form DACA-89-C-0315, while it is possible that in fiscal year 1990 another project would have the contract number DACA-90-C-0315. Another consideration in assigning a project number is the way in which the project will be updated. Some scheduling software requires the user to enter a new project number for each version of the project. In this case, a good

```
FORMB: <ARROW> Delete End Field Header Load Modify Save Print Verify `V I O   363

                        PROJECT SCREEN (PROALL)

Project Number 1_____  Title 2_____
Report Header, 2nd line/left 3_____

Update Number 14    Report Date (1st/next workday) 15_____        Chance 13_

Duration 33__  Days Remaining 34__  Percent Complete 35___   Prior % Comp 36___
Actual/Scheduled Start 3  38_____          Actual/Scheduled Finish 4  42_____

Required Finish 45_____  Float 20__     Remarks 62_____

Original Contract Amount 72_____  Changes 73_____  Forecast Final Amt 74_____
Actual Earnings This Period 75_____    Actual Earnings Prior Periods 76_____
Retainage This Period 77_____          Retainage Prior Periods 78_____
Sales Tax Total 79_____  Sales Tax This Period 80_____  Prior Period 81_____

Activity File Name/Drive # 86___  / 8  Resource 88___  / 8  Calendar 90___  / 9
(if blank, system will name) 9

Resource Category/Multiplier 9  100_   1  102_   1  104_   Other Cat. 105_
```

Figure 3.6. PMS80 project data screen. (PMS80 Project Management Software, Version 6.00. *Courtesy of Pinnell Engineering, Inc.*)

strategy for multiple projects would be to reserve a range of numbers, for example 0100 to 0199, for a single project and its updates. Other types of four-character designations are often used to refer to the month and year of the data date. Hence, the method of assigning a project code should be consistent with the anticipated method of backing-up and maintaining updated schedules.

ENTERING ACTIVITY DATA

Typically, activity information will be entered on another data entry form on the PC screen. Most scheduling systems have capabilities far more comprehensive than just executing a forward or backward pass in the process of calculating schedule dates and float. In order to broaden their customer base, software vendors have included various levels of complexity of data entry. If only the schedule and float are required, the user need only input basic information and no extra (not to be used) information is required. Figures 3.7, 3.8, and 3.9 demonstrate the differences in levels of data entry complexity from the PMS80 and PROMIS system. Figure 3.7 is the "begin-

```
FORME:<Enter> A B Compute D End F K L M N P ^P R S ^S V <F1>=help   Next (   20)
                                                                    Record
                        EASY ACTIVITY SCREEN (ACTEZ)

Number _____       Description _____   Department ___

Duration ___       Days Remaining ___    Percent Complete ___


Prior Activities    ___    ___    ___    ___    ___
Lag/Lead            _   ___  _  ___  _  ___        Other Priors ___   ___


Remarks _____      Work Area ____    Zone __  __

A/E _  Start Date _____

A/L _  Finish Date _____


Contract Amount _____   Cost Code _____   Budgeted Material Quantity _____

 ENTER Record Number and Press <RETURN>.   Or Command Letter from Top Line.
```

Figure 3.7. PMS80 Beginner data entry form. (PMS80 Project Management Software, Version 6.00. *Courtesy of Pinnell Engineering, Inc.*)

ner" data entry form. Figure 3.8 contains additional details, and is the "advanced" data entry form from the PROMIS scheduling system. For every complex schedules, the data entry form shown in Figure 3.9 may be used.

A minimum of three data elements are required for each activity, so that the software can calculate a network.[1] The necessary data elements are the following: the activity identification number, the logical relationship designation, and the activity duration. From these basic data elements, scheduling software can develop powerful tools. In ADM networks, the "i" and "j" node numbers express both the activity identification and the logical relationships of the network. In the PDM schedule, the activity number uniquely identifies the activity. A list of the preceding or succeeding activities is required, however, to specify the logical relationships between activities.

---

[1] In this book, the word network is used interchangeably with the phrase critical path method.

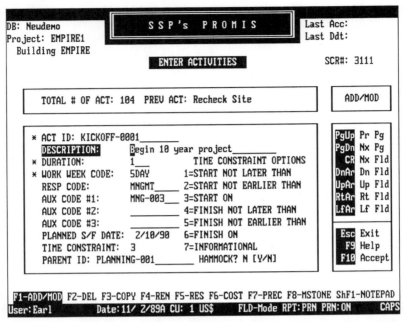

Figure 3.8. PROMIS data entry form. (PROMIS, Version 3.0. *Courtesy of Strategic Software Planning Corp.*)

To maximize the utilization of schedules, clear descriptions for every activity in the network should be entered. Activity durations are typically entered when the activity identification numbers and logical relationships are defined. The following paragraphs will explore some of the effective methods for numbering activities so that effective management tools that can be developed from the data, similar to that required in Figure 3.7, the "beginner" activity data entry screen.

The purpose of the schedule is to provide an effective communication device for construction progress monitoring and control. The depth of this communication is based, initially, on the way that the activities in the schedule are constructed. In most construction projects, there is a natural flow of activities, which occurs by work areas, as well as by trades. This natural flow should always be used to define activities in a schedule.

```
FORME:<Enter> A B Compute D End F K L M N P ^P R S ^S V <F1>=help   Next (   20)
                                                                       Record
                            ACTIVITY SCREEN (ACTALL)

Number _____  Description _____  Department Respon ___

Duration ___ Days Remaining ___  Percent Complete ___    Prior % Complete ___
A/E _ Start Date _____    A/L _ Finish Date _____    Calendar Modifier _

Prior Activities       ___    ___    ___       ___   ___   ___   ___    ___
Lag/Lead           - ____ - ____ - ___   Other Priors ___   ___   Subnet _
Early Start _____  Early Finish _____  Late Start _____  Late Finish _____

Remarks _____    Work Area ____        Zone __ __    _____

Cost Budget _____   Current Cost Estimate _____   Cost Code _____  _____
Actual This Period _____    Actual Prior _____    Contract Amount _____
Budgeted Mat'l Qty _____   This Period Qty _____    Prior Qty _____ Unit ___

Resource Name      ___    ___    ___    ___    ___    ___    ___    ___
Budgeted Quant  _  ___ - _ ___ - _ ___ - _ ___ - _ ___ - _ ___ - _ ___ - _ ___
This Period Qty ____    ____    ____    ____    ____    ____    ____    ____
Prior Quantity  _____   _____   _____   _____   _____   _____   _____   _____

ENTER Record Number and Press <RETURN>.  Or Command Letter from Top Line.
```

Figure 3.9. PMS80 Advanced data entry form. (PMS80 Project Management Software, Version 6.00. *Courtesy of Pinnell Engineering, Inc.*)

The patterns of a schedule can easily be included in an activity's identification number. For example, a typical pattern for mechanical construction tasks that incorporate large equipment may be summarized by the following sequence: submit, owner approval, fabricate and deliver, rough-in, finish, and test. One way to represent these activities, which will enhance communication, is to enforce certain conventions on their identification numbers. For example, in a PDM schedule, all submittal activities could range from 100 to 199, approval activities from 200 to 299, and fabricate and deliver activities from 300 to 399. A similar system could be obtained if the "i" node number of an activity in an ADM network was constructed in the same fashion.

By imposing these numbering conventions, the scheduler can insure, for most small- and medium-sized projects, that the schedule will be understandable at a glance. There will also be a "built-in" schedule analysis tool to help find the activities that may be needed for a specific schedule review later.

More sophisticated levels of conventions may also be built into the activity numbers, depending on the type of project being modeled. For construction projects that have inherently repetitive features, such as multistory building or highway projects, more than one level of sophistication can be incorporated into the activity numbers. Each section of the construction, either a floor of a multistory building or a reach of highway, could have a unique overall coding, such as a specific digit in the thousands column. For example, all second-floor activities might be between "2000" and "2999."

A second level of uniform description could also be included, if similar activities on each floor were coded with the same digits, with a different number in front of it to designate the floor level. For example, all mechanical rough-in could have the number "150"; thus, the third- and fourth-floor mechanical rough-in activity numbers would be "3150" and "4150," respectively.

Combining both types of coding, one for location and the other for type of activity, into a single activity code, is good practice. It promotes clear and concise communication about job progress, and analysis can be accomplished without significant computer time requirements.

Activity descriptions, just as identification numbers, should also facilitate a clear understanding of the physical construction project. The shortened activity description, "DEL REF STL" (for "deliver reinforcing steel"), is a very good example of inappropriate abbreviations for activity descriptions. This type of activity description will not be uniformly understood. Activity descriptions must clearly indicate the nature of the work to be accomplished. For example "DELIVER REBAR" would be a much clearer description than "DEL REF STL."

People unfamiliar with the project, and those who would use different abbreviations, will find clear, English-language descriptions to be a critical factor in their ability to understand the construction plan and/or to reconstruct the actual sequence of construction.

One way in which the scheduling engineer may think of activity descriptions, is to think of any activity as a combination of an action verb, such as approve, deliver, or test, and an object, such as plumbing, duct work, or carpet. Occasionally, these object words may be used to modify other types of objects. For example, a particular activity may be "Approve Electrical Shop Drawings." In addition to using clear language, complete activity descriptions must be used consistently.

Although a complete description would be most effective, occasionally abbreviations are necessary due to the limited field lengths utilized by some programs. In this case, a legend that translates these abbreviations should also be included with any schedule information exchanges.

Another critical factor, when creating a network model of a construction project, is adequate representation of the relationships between the activities. The general standard of practice is to have network activities interact in the same manner as the company's preconceived notion as to how the work will be accomplished. Occasionally, however, the preconceived plan of work does not model the actual physical constraints in the project. This type of plan will have to be revised more frequently than a plan that models physical constraints first and then adds management preferences second.

Members of the project team may also wish to skew the schedule for their own benefit. One common example is to assign longer-than-realistic durations to activities that are expected to be delayed. Once the activity is delayed, the owner will often have to pay more than should be paid to compensate project team members. By making schedules too restrictive in completion or phasing requirements, owners could also skew the schedule in their favor. Insuring, at the start of a project, that activities are properly defined and related is the best insurance against such unethical practices.

When creating a model of a construction project, the scheduler divides the work into spatial areas, such as first and second floors, or east and west wings. Once this is completed, the scheduler can visualize crews moving through those spaces. When one crew moves into a new area, the next crew can move into the vacated space.

While a repetitive construction schedule is very efficient, since it allows the contractor's forces to take advantage of the learning-curve productivity gains, the scheduler may make assumptions that are not valid. One of these assumptions is that all crews operate at the same rate of production in a given area. Unless all crews complete their portion of the project in the same amount of time, some crews will be idle while waiting for others to finish, and the project may lose money. In nonrepetitive projects, such as a rehabilitation of existing facilities, a scheduler needs to develop activities and their relationships by the natural constraints imposed by the facility itself, not by perceived resource allocations. Once this type of schedule is constructed, the scheduler may determine efficient crew levels through resource analysis techniques. Additional discussion of this topic is contained in Chapter 6.

The application of actual construction constraints, and not the generally accepted practice of roughing out a "crew chase[2]," is the most effective way to create an efficient construction schedule. Resource analysis techniques are then employed to determine the most efficient number of workers on the site each day. While some may feel that this amount of effort is unnecessary, real productivity gains can occur at the construction site, using this type of analysis.

Once the schedule has been created, activities are accessed for on-screen viewing and modification by entering the activity's identification number and pressing a key or series of keys, which instructs the program to find and display the activity's information. If, however, a large number of related activities must be viewed or modified, this process is tedious and requires the user to constantly refer to a printed report to find each desired activity identification number. To assist the user in rapidly entering activity information, software vendors have included a number of time-saving features in data retrieval screens.

One example of a time-saving feature is the ability to quickly access activities for updating or modification. The user can select the activities that the contractor has scheduled, beginning with the present date.

Another variation of the multiple activity-access feature is the use of table editors. Table editors allow the user to scroll through and access all activities within a table. This feature, while useful, is not as powerful as searching for particular activities, because the user still must look through the list of all activities prior to locating those required for modification or updating. Some systems, however, allow the selection of a subset of activities in the table format. Figure

---

[2]The way that various resources follow each other through a project is sometimes referred to as a "crew chase."

```
INPUT:<Esc> <Arrows> ^A ^D ^F ^G ^K ^L ^N ^O ^R ^Z ^Utilities <F1>   Record    1
                                                                      Field     2
                       ACTIVITY SCREEN (ACTMR)
 Num Description                 Dep Day Prio r Ac tivi ties Lag/Lead for Zo
 ber                             art Dur 1st 2nd 3rd 4th 1st 3 Priors ne
   1 PROJECT_START_____  OWN 00  ___ ___ ___ ___ _____  10_
   2 SURVEY & SOILS TESTS, 10 HOLES PE1  7   1   ___ ___ ___ _____  +4_
   3 PRELIMINARY DESIGN_____  PE2 11   1   ___ ___ ___ _____  +2_
   4 DESIGN REVIEW & APPROVAL___ OWN  1   3   2   ___ ___ _____  -1_
   5 FINAL DESIGN, PLANS AND SPECS_ PE2 20   4   ___ ___ ___ _____  +1_
   6 NEGOTIATE, AWARD & N.T.P.__ PE2 25   5   ___ ___ ___ _____  ___
   7 DESIGN PHASE_____ PE2 60   3   6   ___ ___  H_____   1_
   8 MOBILIZE_____ GC_ 15   6   ___ ___ ___ _____  ___
   9 SITE EARTHWORK AND UTILITIES__ EX_ 60   6   8   ___ ___    -   5   +8_
  10 REVIEW & APPROVE SHOP DRAWINGS PE2  2   8   ___ ___ ___  S  5     -1_
  11 FORM AND POUR FOOTINGS_____ GC_ 10   8  10   ___ ___    +   5     ___
  12 F & P COLUMNS, BEAMS & SLAB__ GC_ 20  11   ___ ___ ___ _____  ___
  13 SET ROOF BEAMS AND JOISTS___ GC_ 10  12   ___ ___ ___ _____  +2_
  14 ERECT BUILDING SKIN & ROOF__ GC_ 20  12   ___ ___ ___ _____  ___
  15 MECHANICAL, PLUMBING & FIRE__ ME_ 45  12   ___ ___ ___ _____  +4_
  16 ELECTRICAL POWER & CONTROL__ ME_ 40  12   ___ ___ ___ _____  +6_
  17 INSTALL PROCESS EQUIPMENT____ GC_ 60  14  13  16   ___   F  5     ___
  18 CONSTRUCTION PHASE_____ GC_ 130  8  19   ___ ___  H_____   1_
```

Figure 3.10. PMS80 table editor. (PMS80 Project Management Software, Version 6.00. *Courtesy of Pinnell Engineering, Inc.*)

```
SAMPLE                        EDIT RESOURCES              DATE:   30Aug90
Division A               Add New Categories of Resources, or  ROW:      2.2
                         Edit Existing Resource Information.   NETWORK CHART
── PLAN ──── AUTO ──── SAVE ──────────────
┌──────────────────── Resource Information ────────────────────┐
│ Resource Name  │ Resource │ Resource Description │  Expense  │Unit│
│                │ Group    │                      │  Rate     │Msr.│
├────────────────┼──────────┼──────────────────────┼───────────┼────┤
│ Programmer A   │ A0001    │ P. Robinson          │ $  50.00  │Whrs│
│ Programmer B   │ A0001    │ G. Bell              │ $  60.00  │Whrs│
│ Designer A     │ A0001    │ J. Schwartz          │ $  50.00  │Whrs│
│ Designer B     │ A0001    │ K. Elmy              │ $  60.00  │Whrs│
│ Tech Writer A  │ B0001    │ H. Valasquez         │ $  50.00  │Whrs│
│ Tech Writer B  │ B0001    │ J. Spiller           │ $  60.00  │Whrs│
│ Equipment      │ C0001    │                      │ $   1.00  │$   │
│ Misc Expense   │ C0002    │                      │ $   1.00  │$   │
│                │          │                      │ $   0.00  │    │
└────────────────┴──────────┴──────────────────────┴───────────┴────┘
```

Figure 3.11. ViewPoint table editor. (ViewPoint, Version 3.1. *Courtesy of Computer Aided Management, Inc.*)

3.10 shows the PMS80 table editor; Figure 3.11 shows the subset table editor from the ViewPoint scheduling system.

ESTABLISH THE PROJECT WORK CALENDAR

As determined in Chapter 2, the example piping project would take 44 days to complete. What assumptions were made that affect a "real-world" completion of the project in 44 days? The first assumption relates to labor. Construction crews, unless paid overtime, do not work 7 days a week, 24 hours a day. There are certain assumptions that have been included in this 44-day schedule, which need to be understood. It is assumed that the owner does not want any crew to work over 8 hours a day, or to do any weekend work.

Scheduling software provides several tools that allow the user to define the hours of the workday, the days in the workweek, recognized holidays, and specialized calendars for individual labor subgroups.

For the example project, the workday will begin at 7:00 a.m. and will end at 3:30 p.m. While this assumption is very reasonable, it can yield some surprising results. For the unwary user, activities will appear to have durations of one day less than their actual duration. For example, an activity with a three day duration may be shown, in a computer model, as starting on January 10 and completing on January 12. This does not mean, however, that it takes two days to complete the project, it actually takes the entire three full work days, because the completion occurs at the end of the last day. When reviewing a network, the construction staff should remember how workdays are actually calculated in the scheduling software. Some scheduling software also allows for the scheduling of shiftwork over the entire 24-hour period, if round-the-clock production is desired.

Project management software will allow the definition of a work calendar that specifies the days of the week on which activities may post progress. Holidays may also be included in the calendar, to denote days that are not counted when progress is posted to an activity. Additionally, some project management programs allow for the specification of different calendars within one schedule. Figures 3.12 and 3.13 show the data entry screens for holiday and calendar data from the Aldergraf and PPMS scheduling systems.

Variable workweek duration is offered by many scheduling software programs. The systems usually allow the user to provide differ-

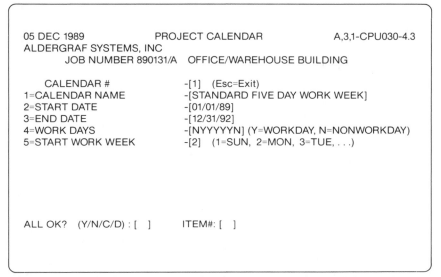

```
05 DEC 1989              PROJECT CALENDAR              A,3,1-CPU030-4.3
ALDERGRAF SYSTEMS, INC
      JOB NUMBER 890131/A   OFFICE/WAREHOUSE BUILDING

      CALENDAR #              -[1]  (Esc=Exit)
   1=CALENDAR NAME            -[STANDARD FIVE DAY WORK WEEK]
   2=START DATE               -[01/01/89]
   3=END DATE                 -[12/31/92]
   4=WORK DAYS                -[NYYYYYN] (Y=WORKDAY, N=NONWORKDAY)
   5=START WORK WEEK          -[2]  (1=SUN, 2=MON, 3=TUE, . . .)




   ALL OK?  (Y/N/C/D) : [   ]      ITEM#: [   ]
```

Figure 3.12. Aldergraf project calendar entry screen. (Aldergraf Scheduling System, Version 4.2/3. *Courtesy of Aldergraf Systems, Inc.*)

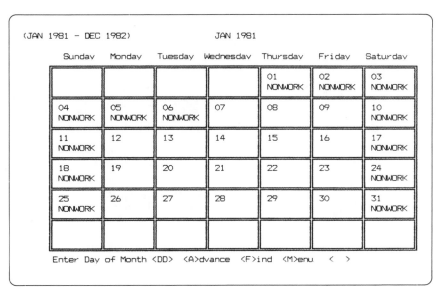

Figure 3.13. PPMS calendar entry screen. (PPMS-30000, Version 3.6. *Courtesy of Advanced Project Analysts*)

ent calendars for different types of crews. While this can be a very powerful tool for a complex job, many projects do not require this feature.

PC scheduling programs typically allow for the selection between five- and seven-day workweek schedules. One is no better than the other, although there is often disagreement on this between project managers. The five-day workweek schedule, Monday through Friday (with Saturday and Sunday off), is the general standard. The five-day workweek does, however, pose a problem if the contractor actually works on a weekend. If weekend work is necessary, new activity completion times are needed. Figure 3.14 shows the effects of the position of the weekend on the number of calendar days required for completion of the example network "Excavation," which has a three-day duration.

Another approach to modeling the working week is by calculating the schedule based on a seven-day workweek, and using "no workdays" for the weekend. These "no workdays" will allow the activity to finish on the same date as the five-day workweek schedule.

The seven-day workweek may also be used to allow a contractor to more easily make up for lost time. However, weekend days are not used by most contractors. Improving productivity during regular hours is the option most often chosen.

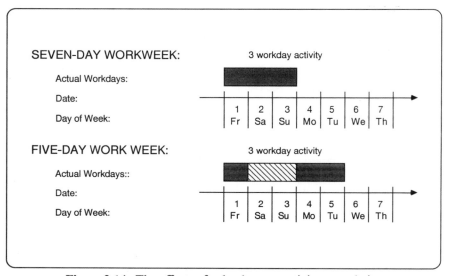

Figure 3.14. The effects of calendars on activity completion.

The example piping schedule has been calculated to illustrate the results of a seven-day calendar and a five-day calendar. As demonstrated in Figure 3.14, significant different project completion dates occur when five- or seven-day workweek calendars are utilized. Table 3.1 uses a seven-day workweek, a workday of 0700 to 1500 hours, and no holidays. Table 3.2 presents a five-day workweek, a workday of 0700 to 1500, and including typical federal holidays. The completion date is 29 Nov 89 for the five-day calendar, and 12 Nov 89 for a seven-day calendar.

The obvious differences in these calculations will lead to major difficulties for the construction office and the contractor if workweeks and holidays are not coordinated prior to the initial submission of a contractor's schedule.

PROJECT PROGRESS

After the construction begins, a contractor will request payment for the progress that has been made to date. For payment, the schedule may be used as a spreadsheet to identify a dollar amount to pay the contractor, based on some measure of completion of each of the activities.

Prior to exploring the way in which scheduling software can be used to analyze progress on the construction site, there are several important technical aspects that must be defined. These include time-based progress, the use of the data date, default calculations, out-of-sequence progress, and fiscal compensation. Time-based progress and the used data date are discussed below. Default calculations and fiscal compensation are covered in the following chapter.

The terminology used for posting progress in the scheduling software is one area that the project management team must agree upon. In addition to term definitions, the methods that the program uses to manipulate this information in order to schedule the project must also be discussed. As with the examples describing the workweek definitions, failure to come to an agreement on these issues may cause the different offices to obtain completely different results from the same "raw" project data.

The percentage of payments made is an essential element in determining the status of a project. This percentage should be a sum of the progress that the contractor has made on each activity. In Table 3.3, for example, it is assumed that a contractor is trying to

Table 3.1. Initial schedule report (seven day/wk).

ACTIVITY/ SUCCESSORS	DESCRIPTION	ORIGINAL DURATION	REMAINING DURATION	EARLY START/FINISH	LATE START/FINISH	FLOAT
1/ 2, 3	Start Job	1	1	2 Oct 89 / 2 Oct 89	2 Oct 89 / 2 Oct 89	0
2/ 10	Relocate Electric	6	6	3 Oct 89 / 8 Oct 89	1 Nov 89 / 6 Nov 89	29
3/ 4	Excavate	3	3	3 Oct 89 / 5 Oct 89	3 Oct 89 / 5 Oct 89	0
4/ 5, 6	Install Pipe Section One	10	10	6 Oct 89 / 15 Oct 89	6 Oct 89 / 15 Oct 89	0
5/ 7	Backfill Section One	5	5	16 Oct 89 / 20 Oct 89	23 Oct 89 / 27 Oct 89	7
6/ 7, 8	Install Pipe Section Two	12	12	16 Oct 89 / 27 Oct 89	16 Oct 89 / 27 Oct 89	0
7/ 9	Backfill Section Two	8	8	28 Oct 89 / 4 Nov 89	28 Oct 89 / 4 Nov 89	0
8/ 9, 10	Test Pipe Sections	3	3	28 Oct 89 / 30 Oct 89	2 Nov 89 / 4 Nov 89	5
9/ 12	Grade & Sod	7	7	5 Nov 89 / 11 Nov 89	5 Nov 89 / 11 Nov 89	0
10/ 11	Install Manhole	3	3	31 Oct 89 / 2 Nov 89	7 Nov 89 / 9 Nov 89	7
11/ 12	Test Electric	2	2	3 Nov 89 / 4 Nov 89	10 Nov 89 / 11 Nov 89	7
12/	Inspect	1	1	12 Nov 89 / 12 Nov 89	12 Nov 89 / 12 Nov 89	0

Table 3.2. Initial Schedule Report (five day/wk + holidays).

ACTIVITY/ SUCCESSORS	DESCRIPTION	ORIGINAL DURATION	REMAINING DURATION	EARLY START/FINISH	LATE START/FINISH	FLOAT
1/2, 3	Start Job	1	1	2 Oct 89 / 2 Oct 89	2 Oct 89 / 2 Oct 89	0
2/10	Relocate Electric	6	6	3 Oct 89 / 10 Oct 89	13 Nov 89 / 20 Nov 89	29
3/4	Excavate	3	3	3 Oct 89 / 5 Oct 89	3 Oct 89 / 5 Oct 89	0
4/5, 6	Install Pipe Section One	10	10	6 Oct 89 / 19 Oct 89	6 Oct 89 / 19 Oct 89	0
5/7	Backfill Section One	5	5	20 Oct 89 / 26 Oct 89	31 Oct 89 / 6 Nov 89	7
6/7, 8	Install Pipe Section Two	12	12	20 Oct 89 / 6 Nov 89	20 Oct 89 / 6 Nov 89	0
7/9	Backfill Section Two	8	8	7 Nov 89 / 16 Nov 89	7 Nov 89 / 16 Nov 89	0
8/9, 10	Test Pipe Sections	3	3	7 Nov 89 / 9 Nov 89	14 Nov 89 / 16 Nov 89	5
9/12	Grade & Sod	7	7	17 Nov 89 / 28 Nov 89	17 Nov 89 / 28 Nov 89	0
10/11	Install Manhole	3	3	10 Nov 89 / 14 Nov 89	21 Nov 89 / 24 Nov 89	7
11/12	Test Electric	2	2	15 Nov 89 / 16 Nov 89	27 Nov 89 / 28 Nov 89	7
12/	Inspect	1	1	29 Nov 89 / 29 Nov 89	29 Nov 89 / 29 Nov 89	0

Table 3.3. Progress data as of November 2, 1989.

ACTIVITY/ SUCCESSORS	DESCRIPTION	ORIGINAL DURATION	REMAINING DURATION	ACTUAL START	ACTUAL FINISH
1/ 2, 3	Start Job	1	0	2 Oct 89	2 Oct 89
2/ 10	Relocate Electric	6	3	9 Oct 89	
3/ 4	Excavate	3	0	5 Oct 89	9 Oct 89
4/ 5, 6	Install Pipe Section One	10	0	12 Oct 89	25 Oct 89
5/ 7	Backfill Section One	5	0	26 Oct 89	1 Nov 89
6/ 7, 8	Install Pipe Section Two	12	6	26 Oct 89	
7/ 9	Backfill Section Two	8	8		
8/ 9, 10	Test Pipe Sections	3	3		
9/ 12	Grade & Sod	7	7		
10/ 11	Install Manhole	3	3		
11/ 12	Test Electric	2	2		
12/	Inspect	1	1		

determine whether he is ahead or behind schedule, based on time alone.

To update the progress schedule, the contractor must first establish the actual start date of an activity, the remaining duration of that activity, and the date that the activity was completed. Table 3.3 provides this information for the example piping project.

The user should first be aware of two dates before any progress analysis may begin. The first and most important date is the point in time that progress is being measured to; this is referred to as the "data date." The second date is the actual day on which the schedule is being updated. Since it is often the case that information entered into scheduling software can be several days to a week old, the user must keep in mind that the data date is the date that the software uses to reschedule updates.

The scheduling software user must understand the way that a system utilizes the data date, the remaining duration, and the actual

Table 3.4. Updated schedule report (November 2, 1989).

ACTIVITY/ SUCCESSORS	DESCRIPTION	ORIGINAL DURATION	REMAINING DURATION	EARLY START/FINISH	LATE START/FINISH	FLOAT
1/ 2, 3	Start Job	1	0	2 Oct 89A	2 Oct 89A	
2/ 10	Relocate Electric	6	3	9 Oct 89A / 6 Nov 89	9 Oct 89A / 24 Nov 89	13
3/ 4	Excavate	3	0	5 Oct 89A	9 Oct 89A	
4/ 5, 6	Install Pipe Section One	10	0	12 Oct 89A	25 Oct 89A	
5/ 7	Backfill Section One	5	0	26 Oct 89A	1 Nov 89A	
6/ 7, 8	Install Pipe Section Two	12	7	26 Oct 89A / 9 Nov 89	9 Nov 89	0
7/ 9	Backfill Section Two	8	8	10 Nov 89 / 21 Nov 89	10 Nov 89 / 21 Nov 89	0
8/ 9, 10	Test Pipe Sections	3	3	10 Nov 89 / 14 Nov 89	17 Nov 89 / 21 Nov 89	5
9/ 12	Grade & Sod	7	7	22 Nov 89 / 1 Dec 89	22 Nov 89 / 1 Dec 89	0
10/ 11	Install Manhole	3	3	15 Nov 89 / 17 Nov 89	27 Nov 89 / 29 Nov 89	7
11/ 12	Test Electric	2	2	20 Nov 89 / 21 Nov 89	30 Nov 89 / 1 Dec 89	7
12/	Inspect	11	11	4 Dec 89 / 4 Dec 89	4 Dec 89 / 4 Dec 89	0

start and finish dates to calculate a schedule. One possible schedule report based on the update progress information from Table 3.3 is shown in Table 3.4. To assist the user in identifying those activities that have progressed, the letter "A" or a special symbol (such as an asterisk "*") is, in most software, placed beside the actual date.

Prior to analyzing the reasons for a project's poor performance (the schedule slipped three working days, during the period 2 Oct 89 to 2 Nov 89), the methods that may be used in calculating these dates will be explained, utilizing several examples. These examples explore the types of problems that might be expected to occur during a progress updating session at any construction field office. It is important to note that, though each "progress" measuring approach is valid, they will provide different answers, since they evaluate different items.

Basically, an activity is "in progress" if the remaining duration time is between the original duration and zero. Although the remaining duration is frequently used as an indication of progress, another method used to describe an activity in progress is the *expended duration*. Expended duration represents the number of days of work already accomplished. This concept corresponds to *earned*

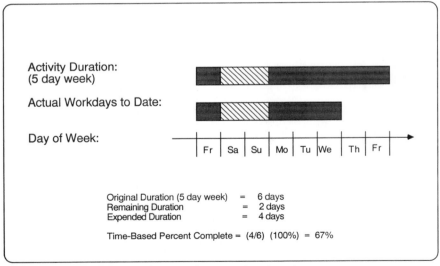

Figure 3.15. Duration and time-based progress.

value, which is explained later in the book. If an activity was ten days long, and had four days of remaining duration, there would be six days of expended duration.

The time-based *percent complete* is an important concept, and is often used addition to, or in place of, remaining or expended duration. In some systems, the percent complete and remaining duration are linked. In these cases, the time-based percent complete is calculated by dividing the expended duration by the original duration. Some systems allow the percent complete and the remaining duration to be independent figures. The relative values of the two durations and the time-based percent complete, for the possible progress conditions, are given in Figure 3.15.

Chapter 4

Practitioner Project Scheduling Topics

INTRODUCTION

Once the basics of entering schedule data and calculating the schedule are learned, the scheduler will need to obtain information to monitor and control job progress. The next section of this chapter, "Turning Data Into Information," illustrates several specific techniques that can be used to efficiently monitor typical construction projects.

The means by which scheduling systems calculate the cost and time of schedules will be explained in the next several sections of this chapter. The section on "Milestones and Target Dates" provides the background necessary to model final and interim completion dates. That on "Default Completion Calculations" explains how scheduling systems may take control of CPM calculations. The section on "Adding Cost Data to Activities" describes the way in which the data for costs and time may be combined to provide a more comprehensive project management tool.

The techniques described in this chapter may be applied to many different types of scheduling systems and projects. Scheduling for all but the most specialized types of construction projects can be tackled by using these techniques.

TURNING DATA INTO INFORMATION

The ability to obtain useful information from schedule data has increased significantly since the early days of CPM scheduling. In the past, scheduling programs only provided a fixed list of reports. These reports typically listed every schedule activity according to the activity numbers, early start dates, and total float. Since one page of the report usually contained a maximum of fifty activities, a 1000-activity schedule would require sixty pages or more to list the activity numbers, early start dates, and total float reports.

While voluminous paper reports provide "hard copy" documentation, they have very limited usefulness for analyzing large amounts of schedule data. Analyzing large stacks of reports requires hours of tracing activity logic from one activity to another, while simultaneously evaluating activity data from several reports. Unless the construction team has sufficient skills and manpower available to analyze these reports, all of the work that went into developing the schedule is lost. The users of scheduling software quickly realize that data analysis is very time-consuming, and often choose to only use the schedule to meet initial contract requirements.

Scheduling software offers many time-saving features. The most important of these features assists the reviewer in rapidly analyzing schedule data, by allowing the reviewer to select activities of interest for each schedule analysis task. The activities of interest for a specific schedule analysis task will, typically, be limited to a small subset of the total number of activities in the network. Reviewing a small subset of activities, rather than the entire schedule, will dramatically increase the efficiency of the schedule reviewer.

In order to turn a large amount of activity data into information that can be analyzed and modified more readily, an effective activity coding scheme is necessary. Several ways of effectively using the activity coding necessary to monitor and control project progress, and various implementations of coding in commercial software, are explained below.

ACTIVITY CODING

In order to obtain a timely and detailed analysis of a construction schedule, the user must first gather information on only those activities that are necessary for the particular analysis. Activity codes can assist the scheduler in selecting specific subsets of activities from large networks, and can be used to sort these activities according to necessary criteria. The ability to "select" and "sort" schedule data by activity codes provides key information on which to base decisions.

Selecting Activities

Selection is the process of creating needed subsets of data from a large database. One familiar example of selecting items out of a large database is that of retail store advertisements. In order to decide who should receive the advertisements, a company begins with a vast database of all potential customers, possibly obtained from a city telephone book. Rather than send advertisements to everyone in the city, the store's marketing director will identify those regions of the city that contain the largest numbers of potential customers. If the marketing director is smart, the regions that have already been identified in the city telephone book by zip codes will be used. In order to gather specific information from a large schedule, the scheduler, like the marketing director, will have to identify the category, or "zip code" that will most likely provide the largest payback. Using a "zip code" is limited, however, because it only allows identification of a geographical region, and not specific residents within that region.

To target activities in a construction schedule for a particular schedule analysis task, an "activity code," similar to a "zip code," must be used. If, for example, a listing of all electrical activities, was required then an activity code that contains the value of the activity's specification section would be needed. Also, the scheduler would need to know which of the values in the specification section activity code relate to electrical work. Other types of useful activity codes are suggested by the following questions:

Are all of the necessary activities included on the first floor of this building?

Are all of the necessary activities included in the exterior closure of this building?

Are all of the owner's approval activities in the schedule?

Which activities where used to justify the time extension for a specific claim?

The ability to select activities becomes very powerful when more than one condition is used to target very specific lists of activities. For example, if it were necessary to identify the first floor electrical activities, then the scheduler would need to select those activities implemented on the first floor, and then more specifically select those activities that contain electrical work. Other types of questions that may be answered by using more than one type of selection are suggested by the following questions:

Is there enough time to approve elevator submittal?

When will the building be enclosed?

What mechanical activities need to be finished in the next two weeks?

Will concrete placement be delayed by weather?

Will all necessary services be connected to the Heating and Air Conditioning prior to the testing of the system?

Activity coding is the most efficient way to check the accuracy or status of a construction schedule. To use activity codes effectively the scheduler must seriously consider how to categorize activities. Table 4.1, below, provides a suggested minimum list of activity codes that should be used in a large construction project.

Sorting Activities

Once a subset of activities has been selected, you need to sort the activities in some useful way. In the advertisement mailing list example, one useful sort would be to alphabetize the list of residents in each zip code. For construction activity subsets, useful sorts often

Table 4.1. Suggested activity codes.

ACTIVITY CODE	DEFINITION
Responsibility	Designation for the trade or subcontractor who is responsible for the work in an activity
Work Area	Designation for a particular area of the work, such as floor number or phase of work, relating to an activity
Type of Activity	Designation for the type of an activity, such as: submittal, approval, deliver, install, test, etc.
Specification	Designation for the construction contract specifications relating to an activity.
Building System	Designation for the building system relating to an activity
Weather Sensitive	Designation for weather-sensitive activity
Mod/Claim Number	Designation for the change order or claim relating to an activity

relate to the activity start or completion dates. Other than using the activity start or completion dates, activities may be sorted by any one of the activity code fields.

In a manner similar to selecting activities, sorting activities may also be accomplished by using more than one code field at a time. Using multiple activity data elements to sort a list of activities is particularly useful with an ADM schedule. Since several activities may have the same "i" node, a report that only sorts by a single data element, for instance the "i" node, could result in a report that randomly lists all activities from each node. A more beneficial report may be obtained if you first sort the list by the "i" node, and then sort the list by the "j" node.

USING ACTIVITY CODES

Activity codes allow you to obtain specific schedule data to answer focused questions about the accuracy of the schedule or project progress. An example from an actual construction schedule will illustrate how activity codes can assist in verifying schedule logic and controlling construction progress. The example project, the Spiral Court Apartments, is a six-story steel-framed apartment building with a wood siding exterior.

There are many questions regarding project progress that are asked on almost every construction project. The following list includes several of these typical questions:

Does the schedule show the project being completed on time?
Are all of the important features of the project included in the schedule?
Is the sequence of construction reasonable?
Are activities that require specific coordination with other members of the construction team included in the schedule?
Are there weather-sensitive activities that occur during poor weather periods?
When should inspections be conducted?
What should the contractor be working on this week?

Table 4.2 shows the initial schedule for the Spiral Court Apartments project. This schedule was calculated with a five day work

Table 4.2. Spiral Court Apartments schedule.

ACTIVITY NUMBER	ORIGINAL DURATION	DESCRIPTION	EARLY START	EARLY FINISH	LATE START	LATE FINISH	FLOAT
1	1	Notice To Proceed	29 MAY 86	29 MAY 86	29 MAY 86	29 MAY 86	0
5	15	Mobilization	2 JUN 86	20 JUN 86	2 JUN 86	20 JUN 86	0
30	60	Submit Structural Steel Drawings	23 JUN 86	16 SEP 86	23 JUN 86	16 SEP 86	0
60	30	Submit Cabinet Drawings	23 JUN 86	4 AUG 86	7 NOV 86	22 DEC 86	97
80	30	Submit Door/Window Schedule	23 JUN 86	4 AUG 86	10 DEC 86	22 JAN 87	118
70	30	Submit Exterior Siding Drawings	23 JUN 86	4 AUG 86	18 DEC 86	30 JAN 87	124
10	16	Excavate	23 JUN 86	15 JUL 86	23 DEC 86	15 JAN 87	127
40	30	Submit Equipment	23 JUN 86	4 AUG 86	7 JAN 87	17 FEB 87	136
90	30	Submit Spiral/Exterior Stairs	23 JUN 86	4 AUG 86	4 FEB 87	17 MAR 87	156
56	150	Procure Furnishings	23 JUN 86	26 JAN 87	10 MAR 87	8 OCT 87	180
15	5	Site Utilities	16 JUL 86	22 JUL 86	16 JAN 87	22 JAN 87	127
20	32	Foundation	23 JUL 86	4 SEP 86	23 JAN 87	9 MAR 87	127
25	17	Drainage and Waterproofing	23 JUL 86	14 AUG 86	25 SEP 87	19 OCT 87	299
63	60	Approve Cabinet Drawings	5 AUG 86	28 OCT 86	23 DEC 86	18 MAR 87	97
83	15	Approve Door/Window Schedule	5 AUG 86	25 AUG 86	23 JAN 87	12 FEB 87	118
73	15	Approve Exterior Siding Drawings	5 AUG 86	25 AUG 86	2 FEB 87	20 FEB 87	124
43	15	Approve Equipment	5 AUG 86	25 AUG 86	18 FEB 87	10 MAR 87	136
93	15	Approve Spiral/Exterior Stairs	5 AUG 86	25 AUG 86	18 MAR 87	7 APR 87	156
735	5	Form and Pour Sidewalk/Drive	15 AUG 86	21 AUG 86	20 OCT 87	26 OCT 87	299
730	1	Handicapped signs	15 AUG 86	15 AUG 86	26 OCT 87	26 OCT 87	303
86	120	Procure Doors and Windows	26 AUG 86	16 FEB 87	13 FEB 87	3 AUG 87	118
76	120	Procure Exterior Siding	26 AUG 86	16 FEB 87	23 FEB 87	11 AUG 87	124
46	120	Procure Equipment	26 AUG 86	16 FEB 87	11 MAR 87	27 AUG 87	136
96	60	Procure Spiral/Exterior Stairs	26 AUG 86	18 NOV 86	8 APR 87	1 JUL 87	156
33	30	Approve Structural Steel	17 SEP 86	28 OCT 86	17 SEP 86	28 OCT 86	0

(continued)

59

Table 4.2. (continued)

ACTIVITY NUMBER	ORIGINAL DURATION	DESCRIPTION	EARLY START	EARLY FINISH	LATE START	LATE FINISH	FLOAT
36	90	Procure Structural Steel	29 OCT 86	9 MAR 87	29 OCT 86	9 MAR 87	0
66	120	Procure Cabinets	29 OCT 86	20 APR 87	19 MAR 87	7 SEP 87	97
100	5	Steel Framing and Pan Forms	10 MAR 87	16 MAR 87	10 MAR 87	16 MAR 87	0
105	16	Place Concrete	17 MAR 87	7 APR 87	17 MAR 87	7 APR 87	0
200	5	Steel Framing and Pan Forms	17 MAR 87	23 MAR 87	1 APR 87	7 APR 87	11
103	1	Steel Exterior Stairs	17 MAR 87	17 MAR 87	21 APR 87	21 APR 87	25
300	5	Steel Framing and Pan Forms	24 MAR 87	30 MAR 87	23 APR 87	29 APR 87	22
203	1	Steel Exterior Stairs	24 MAR 87	24 MAR 87	11 MAY 87	11 MAY 87	34
400	5	Steel Framing and Pan Forms	31 MAR 87	6 APR 87	15 MAY 87	21 MAY 87	33
303	1	Steel Exterior Stairs	31 MAR 87	31 MAR 87	1 JUN 87	1 JUN 87	43
710	1	Install Hoist	31 MAR 87	31 MAR 87	23 OCT 87	23 OCT 87	145
500	5	Steel Framing and Pan Forms	7 APR 87	13 APR 87	9 JUN 87	15 JUN 87	44
403	1	Steel Exterior Stairs	7 APR 87	7 APR 87	19 JUN 87	19 JUN 87	52
205	16	Place Concrete	8 APR 87	29 APR 87	8 APR 87	29 APR 87	0
110	8	Steel Studs	8 APR 87	17 APR 87	22 APR 87	1 MAY 87	10
120	7	Electrical Rough-in	10 APR 87	20 APR 87	29 JUN 87	8 JUL 87	55
115	5	Wall Insulation	10 APR 87	16 APR 87	1 JUL 87	8 JUL 87	57
130	4	Interior Spiral Steel Stairs	10 APR 87	15 APR 87	2 JUL 87	8 JUL 87	58
600	5	Steel Framing and Pan Forms	14 APR 87	20 APR 87	1 JUL 87	8 JUL 87	55
503	1	Steel Exterior Stairs	14 APR 87	14 APR 87	10 JUL 87	10 JUL 87	61
125	14	Mechanical Rough-in	15 APR 87	4 MAY 87	29 APR 87	18 MAY 87	10
603	1	Steel Exterior Stairs	21 APR 87	21 APR 87	30 JUL 87	30 JUL 87	70
305	16	Place Concrete	30 APR 87	21 MAY 87	30 APR 87	21 MAY 87	0
210	8	Steel Studs	30 APR 87	11 MAY 87	12 MAY 87	21 MAY 87	8

220	7	Electrical Rough-in	4 MAY 87	12 MAY 87	9 JUL 87	17 JUL 87	46
215	5	Wall Insulation	4 MAY 87	8 MAY 87	13 JUL 87	17 JUL 87	48
230	4	Interior Spiral Steel Stairs	4 MAY 87	7 MAY 87	14 JUL 87	17 JUL 87	49
135	7	Install and Finish Dry wall	5 MAY 87	13 MAY 87	9 JUL 87	17 JUL 87	45
225	14	Mechanical Rough-in	7 MAY 87	26 MAY 87	19 MAY 87	8 JUN 87	8
140	8	Doors and Hardware	7 MAY 87	18 MAY 87	4 AUG 87	13 AUG 87	61
150	8	Exterior Siding	7 MAY 87	18 MAY 87	12 AUG 87	21 AUG 87	67
145	5	Paint	14 MAY 87	20 MAY 87	15 SEP 87	21 SEP 87	85
155	6	Appliances and Furnace	19 MAY 87	26 MAY 87	28 AUG 87	7 SEP 87	71
165	3	Bathroom/Kitchen Cabinets	19 MAY 87	21 MAY 87	8 SEP 87	10 SEP 87	77
175	5	Finish Electrical	19 MAY 87	25 MAY 87	11 SEP 87	17 SEP 87	80
405	16	Place Concrete	22 MAY 87	15 JUN 87	22 MAY 87	15 JUN 87	0
310	8	Steel Studs	22 MAY 87	3 JUN 87	2 JUN 87	11 JUN 87	6
170	5	Finish Plumbing	22 MAY 87	28 MAY 87	11 SEP 87	17 SEP 87	77
320	7	Electrical Rough-in	26 MAY 87	4 JUN 87	20 JUL 87	28 JUL 87	37
315	5	Wall Insulation	26 MAY 87	2 JUN 87	22 JUL 87	28 JUL 87	39
330	4	Interior Spiral Steel Stairs	26 MAY 87	1 JUN 87	23 JUL 87	28 JUL 87	40
235	7	Install and Finish Drywall	27 MAY 87	5 JUN 87	20 JUL 87	28 JUL 87	36
160	3	Floor and Trim	27 MAY 87	1 JUN 87	29 SEP 87	1 OCT 87	86
325	14	Mechanical Rough-in	1 JUN 87	18 JUN 87	9 JUN 87	26 JUN 87	6
240	8	Doors and Hardware	1 JUN 87	10 JUN 87	14 AUG 87	25 AUG 87	53
250	8	Exterior Siding	1 JUN 87	10 JUN 87	24 AUG 87	2 SEP 87	59
180	2	Install Furnishings	2 JUN 87	3 JUN 87	9 OCT 87	12 OCT 87	91
245	5	Paint	8 JUN 87	12 JUN 87	22 SEP 87	28 SEP 87	74
255	6	Appliances and Furnace	11 JUN 87	18 JUN 87	8 SEP 87	15 SEP 87	61
265	3	Bathroom/Kitchen Cabinets	11 JUN 87	15 JUN 87	15 SEP 87	17 SEP 87	66
275	5	Finish Electrical	11 JUN 87	17 JUN 87	18 SEP 87	24 SEP 87	69
505	16	Place Concrete	16 JUN 87	8 JUL 87	16 JUN 87	8 JUL 87	0
410	8	Steel Studs	16 JUN 87	25 JUN 87	22 JUN 87	1 JUL 87	4

(continued)

Table 4.2. (continued)

ACTIVITY NUMBER	ORIGINAL DURATION	DESCRIPTION	EARLY START	EARLY FINISH	LATE START	LATE FINISH	FLOAT
270	5	Finish Plumbing	16 JUN 87	22 JUN 87	18 SEP 87	24 SEP 87	66
420	7	Electrical Rough-in	18 JUN 87	26 JUN 87	29 JUL 87	6 AUG 87	28
415	5	Wall Insulation	18 JUN 87	24 JUN 87	31 JUL 87	6 AUG 87	30
430	4	Interior Spiral Steel Stairs	18 JUN 87	23 JUN 87	3 AUG 87	6 AUG 87	31
335	7	Install and Finish Drywall	19 JUN 87	29 JUN 87	29 JUL 87	6 AUG 87	27
260	3	Floor and Trim	19 JUN 87	23 JUN 87	2 OCT 87	6 OCT 87	73
425	14	Mechanical Rough-in	23 JUN 87	13 JUL 87	29 JUN 87	17 JUL 87	4
340	8	Doors and Hardware	23 JUN 87	2 JUL 87	26 AUG 87	7 SEP 87	45
350	8	Exterior Siding	23 JUN 87	2 JUL 87	3 SEP 87	15 SEP 87	51
280	2	Install Furnishings	24 JUN 87	25 JUN 87	13 OCT 87	14 OCT 87	77
345	5	Paint	30 JUN 87	7 JUL 87	29 SEP 87	5 OCT 87	63
355	6	Appliances and Furnace	6 JUL 87	13 JUL 87	16 SEP 87	23 SEP 87	51
365	3	Bathroom/Kitchen Cabinets	6 JUL 87	8 JUL 87	22 SEP 87	24 SEP 87	55
375	5	Finish Electrical	6 JUL 87	10 JUL 87	25 SEP 87	1 OCT 87	58
605	16	Place Concrete	9 JUL 87	30 JUL 87	9 JUL 87	30 JUL 87	0
510	8	Steel Studs	9 JUL 87	20 JUL 87	13 JUL 87	22 JUL 87	2
370	5	Finish Plumbing	9 JUL 87	15 JUL 87	25 SEP 87	1 OCT 87	55
520	7	Electrical Rough-in	13 JUL 87	21 JUL 87	7 AUG 87	17 AUG 87	19
515	5	Wall Insulation	13 JUL 87	17 JUL 87	11 AUG 87	17 AUG 87	21
530	4	Interior Spiral Steel Stairs	13 JUL 87	16 JUL 87	12 AUG 87	17 AUG 87	22
435	7	Install and Finish Drywall	14 JUL 87	22 JUL 87	7 AUG 87	17 AUG 87	18
360	3	Floor and Trim	14 JUL 87	16 JUL 87	7 OCT 87	9 OCT 87	60
525	14	Mechanical Rough-in	16 JUL 87	4 AUG 87	20 JUL 87	6 AUG 87	2
440	8	Doors and Hardware	16 JUL 87	27 JUL 87	8 SEP 87	17 SEP 87	37
450	8	Exterior Siding	16 JUL 87	27 JUL 87	16 SEP 87	25 SEP 87	43

	Activity	Dur.					
380	Install Furnishings	2	17 JUL 87	20 JUL 87	15 OCT 87	16 OCT 87	63
445	Paint	5	23 JUL 87	29 JUL 87	6 OCT 87	12 OCT 87	52
455	Appliances and Furnace	6	28 JUL 87	4 AUG 87	24 SEP 87	1 OCT 87	41
465	Bathroom/Kitchen Cabinets	3	28 JUL 87	30 JUL 87	29 SEP 87	1 OCT 87	44
475	Finish Electrical	5	28 JUL 87	3 AUG 87	2 OCT 87	8 OCT 87	47
610	Steel Studs	8	31 JUL 87	11 AUG 87	31 JUL 87	11 AUG 87	0
470	Finish Plumbing	5	31 JUL 87	6 AUG 87	2 OCT 87	8 OCT 87	44
620	Electrical Rough-in	7	4 AUG 87	12 AUG 87	18 AUG 87	26 AUG 87	10
615	Wall Insulation	5	4 AUG 87	10 AUG 87	20 AUG 87	26 AUG 87	12
630	Interior Spiral Steel Stairs	4	4 AUG 87	7 AUG 87	21 AUG 87	26 AUG 87	13
535	Install and Finish Drywall	7	5 AUG 87	13 AUG 87	18 AUG 87	26 AUG 87	9
460	Floor and Trim	3	5 AUG 87	7 AUG 87	12 OCT 87	14 OCT 87	47
625	Mechanical Rough-in	14	7 AUG 87	26 AUG 87	7 AUG 87	26 AUG 87	0
540	Doors and Hardware	8	7 AUG 87	18 AUG 87	18 SEP 87	29 SEP 87	29
550	Exterior siding	8	7 AUG 87	18 AUG 87	28 SEP 87	7 OCT 87	35
480	Install Furnishings	2	10 AUG 87	11 AUG 87	19 OCT 87	20 OCT 87	49
700	Roof Sheathing	8	12 AUG 87	21 AUG 87	7 OCT 87	16 OCT 87	39
545	Paint	5	14 AUG 87	20 AUG 87	13 OCT 87	19 OCT 87	41
555	Appliances and Furnace	6	19 AUG 87	26 AUG 87	2 OCT 87	9 OCT 87	31
565	Bathroom/Kitchen Cabinets	3	19 AUG 87	21 AUG 87	6 OCT 87	8 OCT 87	33
575	Finish Electrical	5	19 AUG 87	25 AUG 87	9 OCT 87	15 OCT 87	36
570	Finish Plumbing	5	24 AUG 87	28 AUG 87	9 OCT 87	15 OCT 87	33
705	Shingles and Roofing Tiles	6	24 AUG 87	31 AUG 87	19 OCT 87	26 OCT 87	39
635	Install and Finish Drywall	7	27 AUG 87	7 SEP 87	27 AUG 87	7 SEP 87	0
560	Floor and Trim	3	27 AUG 87	31 AUG 87	15 OCT 87	19 OCT 87	34
640	Doors and Hardware	8	31 AUG 87	10 SEP 87	30 SEP 87	9 OCT 87	21
650	Exterior Siding	8	31 AUG 87	10 SEP 87	8 OCT 87	19 OCT 87	27
580	Install Furnishings	2	1 SEP 87	2 SEP 87	21 OCT 87	22 OCT 87	35
715	Elevator	34	8 SEP 87	23 OCT 87	8 SEP 87	23 OCT 87	0

(continued)

Table 4.2. (continued)

ACTIVITY NUMBER	ORIGINAL DURATION	DESCRIPTION	EARLY START	EARLY FINISH	LATE START	LATE FINISH	FLOAT
645	5	Paint	8 SEP 87	14 SEP 87	20 OCT 87	26 OCT 87	30
655	6	Appliances and Furnace	11 SEP 87	18 SEP 87	12 OCT 87	19 OCT 87	21
665	3	Bathroom/Kitchen Cabinets	11 SEP 87	15 SEP 87	13 OCT 87	15 OCT 87	22
675	5	Finish Electrical	11 SEP 87	17 SEP 87	16 OCT 87	22 OCT 87	25
670	5	Finish Plumbing	16 SEP 87	22 SEP 87	16 OCT 87	22 OCT 87	22
740	1	Test Electrical	18 SEP 87	18 SEP 87	26 OCT 87	26 OCT 87	26
660	3	Floor and Trim	21 SEP 87	23 SEP 87	20 OCT 87	22 OCT 87	21
745	1	Test Mechanical	23 SEP 87	23 SEP 87	26 OCT 87	26 OCT 87	23
680	2	Install Furnishings	24 SEP 87	25 SEP 87	23 OCT 87	26 OCT 87	21
720	1	Remove Hoist	26 OCT 87	26 OCT 87	26 OCT 87	26 OCT 87	0
750	1	Final Inspection	27 OCT 87	27 OCT 87	27 OCT 87	27 OCT 87	0

week and five holidays. The holidays used were *Memorial Day, Independence Day, Labor Day, Thanksgiving,* and *Christmas.* Notice to proceed for the project was issued on May 29, 1986. The contractual project completion was October 27, 1987.

Does the schedule show the project ending by the contract completion date?

Table 4.2 may be used to find the answer. However, you will need to search through all of the pages of the report to locate the activity with the latest finish date. In Table 4.2, the activity that completes the network is on the last page of the schedule. However, this may not always be the case. Most project scheduling systems do not require that activity numbers be sequential. An alternative to flipping through stacks of paper is to develop a report that "targets" activities on the critical path.

The way to obtain the needed report is to select activities with the least float. You may also want to check other activities within a few weeks of the critical path. Checking the near-critical activities will support your efforts to anticipate problems before they delay the project. To obtain this report, simply list all activities with a total float of less than several days from critical. For example, if the critical path has a float of zero days, then you may wish to list all activities that have less than two weeks of float. In the Spiral Court project, since a five-day workweek is used, you would select activities with less than eleven days of float. The output of this selection is shown in Table 4.3.

Perhaps the most efficient way to determine the completion date would be to generate a list of all activities by early finish, sorted with the latest date at the top of the first page. This type of sort is typically referred to as a *descending order* sort. If this report is displayed on the computer's monitor, the last activity in the schedule can be quickly identified.

Are all important features of the project included in the schedule?

If a scheduler only used a report sorted by activity numbers, such as that in Table 4.2, arriving at an answer to this question would be a

Table 4.3. Critical and near-critical activities.

ACTIVITY NUMBER	ORIGINAL DURATION	DESCRIPTION	EARLY START	EARLY FINISH	LATE START	LATE FINISH	FLOAT
1	1	Notice To Proceed	29 MAY 86	29 MAY 86	29 MAY 86	29 MAY 86	0
5	15	Mobilization	2 JUN 86	20 JUN 86	2 JUN 86	20 JUN 86	0
30	60	Submit Structural Steel Drawings	23 JUN 86	16 SEP 86	23 JUN 86	16 SEP 86	0
33	30	Approve Structural Steel	17 SEP 86	28 OCT 86	17 SEP 86	28 OCT 86	0
36	90	Procure Structural Steel	29 OCT 86	9 MAR 87	29 OCT 86	9 MAR 87	0
100	5	Steel Framing and Pan Forms	10 MAR 87	16 MAR 87	10 MAR 87	16 MAR 87	0
105	16	Place Concrete	17 MAR 87	7 APR 87	17 MAR 87	7 APR 87	0
205	16	Place Concrete	8 APR 87	29 APR 87	8 APR 87	29 APR 87	0
110	8	Steel Studs	8 APR 87	17 APR 87	22 APR 87	1 MAY 87	10
125	14	Mechanical Rough-in	15 APR 87	4 MAY 87	29 APR 87	18 MAY 87	10
305	16	Place Concrete	30 APR 87	21 MAY 87	30 APR 87	21 MAY 87	0
210	8	Steel Studs	30 APR 87	11 MAY 87	12 MAY 87	21 MAY 87	8
225	14	Mechanical Rough-in	7 MAY 87	26 MAY 87	19 MAY 87	8 JUN 87	8

Activity	Duration	Description	Early Start	Early Finish	Late Start	Late Finish	Float
405	16	Place Concrete	22 MAY 87	15 JUN 87	22 MAY 87	15 JUN 87	0
310	8	Steel Studs	22 MAY 87	3 JUN 87	2 JUN 87	11 JUN 87	6
325	14	Mechanical Rough-in	1 JUN 87	18 JUN 87	9 JUN 87	26 JUN 87	6
505	16	Place Concrete	16 JUN 87	8 JUL 87	16 JUN 87	8 JUL 87	0
410	8	Steel Studs	16 JUN 87	25 JUN 87	22 JUN 87	1 JUL 87	4
425	14	Mechanical Rough-in	23 JUN 87	13 JUL 87	29 JUN 87	17 JUL 87	4
605	16	Place Concrete	9 JUL 87	30 JUL 87	9 JUL 87	30 JUL 87	0
510	8	Steel Studs	9 JUL 87	20 JUL 87	13 JUL 87	22 JUL 87	2
525	14	Mechanical Rough-in	16 JUL 87	4 AUG 87	20 JUL 87	6 AUG 87	2
610	8	Steel Studs	31 JUL 87	11 AUG 87	31 JUL 87	11 AUG 87	0
620	7	Electrical Rough-in	4 AUG 87	12 AUG 87	18 AUG 87	26 AUG 87	10
535	7	Install and Finish Drywall	5 AUG 87	13 AUG 87	18 AUG 87	26 AUG 87	9
625	14	Mechanical Rough-in	7 AUG 87	26 AUG 87	7 AUG 87	26 AUG 87	0
635	7	Install and Finish Drywall	27 AUG 87	7 SEP 87	27 AUG 87	7 SEP 87	0
715	34	Install Elevator	8 SEP 87	23 OCT 87	8 SEP 87	23 OCT 87	0
720	1	Remove Hoist	26 OCT 87	26 OCT 87	26 OCT 87	26 OCT 87	0
750	1	Final Inspection	27 OCT 87	27 OCT 87	27 OCT 87	27 OCT 87	0

very tedious process. Project scheduling systems, while not being able to directly answer this question, may provide the information needed to make a judgement on the accuracy and completeness of the schedule within minutes, by using activity codes.

For many projects, it may be quickly determined whether all important features of the work have been included in the schedule by selecting activities according to the Work Area code. Using the Work Area code, specific portions of the work may be selected and checked against the required tasks to be performed. Table 4.4 provides a list of all of the activities on the first floor, using the Work Area code. The list is also sorted according to the specification section of the activity using the Construction Specification Index (CSI).

On more complex projects, there are typically activities that require special attention due to their potential impact on project completion. In a hospital, for example, the equipment to be installed is very specialized, and often creates problems during construction. Therefore, one item that should be checked on any hospital project is the specific identification of this equipment on the schedule. The review is conducted by comparing the contract requirements for the hospital equipment with the schedule's activities that concern this equipment. To indicate that an activity is hospital equipment, or some other type of activity, an activity code may be used. By using a standard coding scheme, such as the UCI, any scheduler may select required activities, using standard codes. Once these activities have been identified, it may be rapidly determined whether the schedule is reasonable or requires revision.

Is the sequence of construction reasonable?

The first method that can be used to answer this question is by comparing repetitive activities. Another frequently used method is that of reviewing activities within classes of building systems.

In many projects, there are sets of activities repeated through different work areas of the project. These sets of activities are called "repetitive activities." In the Spiral Court Apartment project, as with many other types of projects, there is a specific sequence of activities that is repeated for every floor. The list of activities on one floor was shown in Table 4.4. This list was developed with the use of

Table 4.4. Use of the Work Area code.

ACTIVITY NUMBER	ORIGINAL DURATION	DESCRIPTION	EARLY START	EARLY FINISH	LATE START	LATE FINISH	FLOAT
100	5	Steel Framing and Pan Forms	10 MAR 87	16 MAR 87	10 MAR 87	16 MAR 87	0
103	1	Steel Exterior Stairs	17 MAY 87	17 MAR 87	21 APR 87	21 APR 87	25
105	16	Place Concrete	17 MAR 87	7 APR 87	17 MAR 87	7 APR 87	0
110	8	Steel Studs	8 APR 87	17 APR 87	22 APR 87	1 MAY 87	10
115	5	Wall Insulation	10 APR 87	16 APR 87	1 JUL 87	8 JUL 87	57
120	7	Electrical Rough-in	10 APR 87	20 APR 87	29 JUN 87	8 JUL 87	55
125	14	Mechanical Rough-in	15 APR 87	4 MAY 87	29 APR 87	18 MAY 87	10
130	4	Interior Spiral Steel Stairs	10 APR 87	15 APR 87	2 JUL 87	8 JUL 87	58
135	7	Install and Finish Dry Wall	5 MAY 87	13 MAY 87	9 JUL 87	17 JUL 87	45
140	8	Doors and Hardware	7 MAY 87	18 MAY 87	4 AUG 87	13 AUG 87	61
145	5	Paint	14 MAY 87	20 MAY 87	15 SEP 87	21 SEP 87	85
150	8	Exterior Siding	7 MAY 87	18 MAY 87	12 AUG 87	21 AUG 87	67
155	6	Appliances and Furnace	19 MAY 87	26 MAY 87	28 AUG 87	7 SEP 87	71
160	3	Floor and Trim	27 MAY 87	1 JUN 87	29 SEP 87	1 OCT 87	86
165	3	Bathroom/Kitchen Cabinets	19 MAY 87	21 MAY 87	8 SEP 87	10 SEP 87	77
170	5	Finish Plumbing	22 MAY 87	28 MAY 87	11 SEP 87	17 SEP 87	77
175	5	Finish Electrical	19 MAY 87	25 MAY 87	11 SEP 87	17 SEP 87	80
180	2	Install Furnishings	2 JUN 87	3 JUN 87	9 OCT 87	12 OCT 87	91

the Work Area code. The first floor activities fall between 100 and 180, with successively higher floors increasing their activity numbers by 100 for each floor.

Using the Work Area codes as a selection criteria, sections of project data may be compared to each other. Those activities that do not match may merit further review. The use of the Work Area code to check patterns of repetitive activities is one way in which a reviewer may check a schedule for an unfamiliar project. On an unfamiliar project, a scheduler will not understand all of the details of the project, but can check the overall logic by reviewing the repetitive activities in similar work areas.

Another means of analyzing the schedule to ensure a logical construction sequence is to select those activities that fit within a building system, such as "Structural." The Building Systems Index (BSI)[1] provides a coding scheme that may be used to categorize activities into types of building systems. With the BSI, for example, a reviewer could determine whether the activities necessary to complete the exterior closure are included. The use of BSI code is important, because BSI cuts across many specification sections of the UCI coding scheme. Table 4.5 lists those activities coded as structural activities.

Using the BSI also allows the creation of a mental model of the process used to complete the project. Understanding the process of the construction plan helps to anticipate problems in crew productivity and conflicts in work area access between different trades.

Are activities that require specific coordination with other members of the construction team included in the schedule?

By selecting activities according to another type of code scheme, the answer may be quickly obtained. One of the activity codes schemes, "TYPE," provides a value for the designation of approval activities. Since these activities will be transmitted to, and reviewed by, several members of the construction team, a coordinated review of the

---

[1]"Computer Aided Cost Estimating System, Control Estimate Generator Users' Manual," U.S. Army Corps of Engineers, Huntsville District, CEHNDSP 88-219, 30 Sep 1988, Appendix G.

Table 4.5. Structural activities.

ACTIVITY NUMBER	ORIGINAL DURATION	DESCRIPTION	EARLY START	EARLY FINISH	LATE START	LATE FINISH	FLOAT
30	60	Structural Steel Drawings	23 JUN 86	16 SEP 86	23 JUN 86	16 SEP 86	0
90	30	Spiral/Exterior Stairs	23 JUN 86	4 AUG 86	4 FEB 87	17 MAR 87	156
93	15	Approve Spiral/Exterior Stairs	5 AUG 86	25 AUG 86	18 MAR 87	7 APR 87	156
96	60	Procure Spiral/Exterior Stairs	26 AUG 86	18 NOV 86	8 APR 87	1 JUL 87	156
33	30	Approve Structural Steel	17 SEP 86	28 OCT 86	17 SEP 86	28 OCT 86	0
36	90	Procure Structural Steel	29 OCT 86	9 MAR 87	29 OCT 86	9 MAR 87	0
100	5	Steel Framing and Pan Forms	10 MAR 87	16 MAR 87	10 MAR 87	16 MAR 87	0
105	16	Place Concrete	17 MAR 87	7 APR 87	17 MAR 87	7 APR 87	0
200	5	Steel Framing and Pan Forms	17 MAR 87	23 MAR 87	1 APR 87	7 APR 87	11
103	1	Steel Exterior Stairs	17 MAR 87	17 MAR 87	21 APR 87	21 APR 87	25
300	5	Steel Framing and Pan Forms	24 MAR 87	30 MAR 87	23 APR 87	29 APR 87	22
203	1	Steel Exterior Stairs	24 MAR 87	24 MAR 87	11 MAY 87	11 MAY 87	34
400	5	Steel Framing and Pan Forms	31 MAR 87	6 APR 87	15 MAY 87	21 MAY 87	33
303	1	Steel Exterior Stairs	31 MAR 87	31 MAR 87	1 JUN 87	1 JUN 87	43
500	5	Steel Framing and Pan Forms	7 APR 87	13 APR 87	9 JUN 87	15 JUN 87	44
403	1	Steel Exterior Stairs	7 APR 87	7 APR 87	19 JUN 87	19 JUN 87	52
205	16	Place Concrete	8 APR 87	29 APR 87	8 APR 87	29 APR 87	0
110	8	Steel Studs	8 APR 87	17 APR 87	22 APR 87	1 MAY 87	10
130	4	Interior Spiral Steel Stairs	10 APR 87	15 APR 87	2 JUL 87	8 JUL 87	58
600	5	Steel Framing and Pan Forms	14 APR 87	20 APR 87	1 JUL 87	8 JUL 87	55
503	1	Steel Exterior Stairs	14 APR 87	14 APR 87	10 JUL 87	10 JUL 87	61
603	1	Steel Exterior Stairs	21 APR 87	21 APR 87	30 JUL 87	30 JUL 87	70
305	16	Place Concrete	30 APR 87	21 MAY 87	30 APR 87	21 MAY 87	0
210	8	Steel Studs	30 APR 87	11 MAY 87	12 MAY 87	21 MAY 87	8
230	4	Interior Spiral Steel Stairs	4 MAY 87	7 MAY 87	14 JUL 87	17 JUL 87	49

(continued)

Table 4.5. (continued)

ACTIVITY NUMBER	ORIGINAL DURATION	DESCRIPTION	EARLY START	EARLY FINISH	LATE START	LATE FINISH	FLOAT
405	16	Place Concrete	22 MAY 87	15 JUN 87	22 MAY 87	15 JUN 87	0
310	8	Steel Studs	22 MAY 87	3 JUN 87	2 JUN 87	11 JUN 87	6
330	4	Interior Spiral Steel Stairs	26 MAY 87	1 JUN 87	23 JUL 87	28 JUL 87	40
505	16	Place Concrete	16 JUN 87	8 JUL 87	16 JUN 87	8 JUL 87	0
410	8	Steel Studs	16 JUN 87	25 JUN 87	22 JUN 87	1 JUL 87	4
430	4	Interior Spiral Steel Stairs	18 JUN 87	23 JUN 87	3 AUG 87	6 AUG 87	31
605	16	Place Concrete	9 JUL 87	30 JUL 87	9 JUL 87	30 JUL 87	0
510	8	Steel Studs	9 JUL 87	20 JUL 87	13 JUL 87	22 JUL 87	2
530	4	Interior Spiral Steel Stairs	13 JUL 87	16 JUL 87	12 AUG 87	17 AUG 87	22
610	8	Steel Studs	31 JUL 87	11 AUG 87	31 JUL 87	11 AUG 87	0
630	4	Interior Spiral Steel Stairs	4 AUG 87	7 AUG 87	21 AUG 87	26 AUG 87	13

approval activities is critical to a successful project. Table 4.6 is a report of the owner's approval activities based on the TYPE code field.

With this report, an owner may also check to see whether all necessary shop drawings have been incorporated into the schedule. In addition, the owner may be able to estimate the resources required to review the shop drawings. The construction contractor may also use this list of approval activities to verify that the owner's approvals are on schedule. Since a frequent construction problem is the untimely submission and approval of shop drawings, this report will prove to be very useful.

Some members of the construction industry object to the inclusion of shop drawing and procurement-related activities in a construction schedule. One of the favorite arguments used is that including the submittal activities in a network creates a schedule that is too big to manage. However, because the procurement process must precede many construction activities, and is often a coordinated effort among various members of the construction team, major procurement activities should be included in the schedule.

There are two methods for making the addition of these activities manageable. The first is to include only those sets of activities for items that take longer than 60 days to manufacture. Secondly, the use of code fields, such as the TYPE field, will allow the combination of approval, procurement, and installation activities on the same schedule, without the need to see all of these activities, unless necessary for a specific review.

To insure that all of the proper submittal activities are in the schedule, the same code field that identifies owner approval activities, "TYPE," may be used to find all of the submittal activities. Table 4.7 is a report of all submittal activities in the example project.

Are there weather-sensitive activities that occur during poor weather periods?

This question can also be solved with activity codes. Rather than the code's value being an abbreviation of a word, the weather-sensitive code is a "logical" code field. Logical code fields refer to codes that may have only two values, for example, "true" or "false," or "yes"

Table 4.6. Approval activities.

ACTIVITY NUMBER	ORIGINAL DURATION	DESCRIPTION	EARLY START	EARLY FINISH	LATE START	LATE FINISH	FLOAT
63	60	Approve Cabinet Drawings	5 AUG 86	28 OCT 86	23 DEC 86	18 MAR 87	97
83	15	Approve Door/Window Schedule	5 AUG 86	25 AUG 86	23 JAN 87	12 FEB 87	118
73	15	Approve Exterior Siding Drawings	5 AUG 86	25 AUG 86	2 FEB 87	20 FEB 87	124
43	15	Approve Equipment	5 AUG 86	25 AUG 86	18 FEB 87	10 MAR 87	136
93	15	Approve Spiral/Exterior Stairs	5 AUG 86	25 AUG 86	18 MAR 87	7 APR 87	156
33	30	Approve Structural Steel	17 SEP 86	28 OCT 86	17 SEP 86	28 OCT 86	0
750	1	Final Inspection	27 OCT 87	27 OCT 87	27 OCT 87	27 OCT 87	0

Table 4.7. Submittal activities.

ACTIVITY NUMBER	ORIGINAL DURATION	DESCRIPTION	EARLY START	EARLY FINISH	LATE START	LATE FINISH	FLOAT
30	60	Submit Structural Steel Drawings	23 JUN 86	16 SEP 86	23 JUN 86	16 SEP 86	0
60	30	Submit Cabinet Drawings	23 JUN 86	4 AUG 86	7 NOV 86	22 DEC 86	97
80	30	Submit Door/Window Schedule	23 JUN 86	4 AUG 86	10 DEC 86	22 JAN 87	118
70	30	Submit Exterior Siding Drawings	23 JUN 86	4 AUG 86	18 DEC 86	30 JAN 87	124
40	30	Submit Equipment	23 JUN 86	4 AUG 86	7 JAN 87	17 FEB 87	136
90	30	Submit Spiral/Exterior Stairs	23 JUN 86	4 AUG 86	4 FEB 87	17 MAR 87	156

or "no." Another interesting feature of this type of coding is that the user only needs to enter one or the other of these values, since a blank may represent the other. If, for example, there are 300 activities in the network, and there are 35 weather-sensitive activities, then only those 35 would have to be coded. The other 265 activities could be blank, which would mean that the activity is not weather sensitive.

Coding for weather sensitivity may be a very important feature, not only in the original review of the schedule, but also after construction begins. As the project proceeds, the original plan may be modified. The impact of the actual progress must be assessed to limit potential problems that may occur later on the job. Moving weather-sensitive activities into a bad weather period is a problem that should be avoided if possible, and this condition may be easily identified if weather-sensitive activity codes are used.

Once this coding scheme is in place, the reviewer could select those activities that have the weather-sensitive coding and then, from that reduced group, print only those activities with start dates between bad weather periods.

A less-sophisticated approach to answering the same question is to obtain a report listing activities according to their BSI code values. Under BSI, rapid identification of those building systems that are typically weather sensitive is possible (foundations, for example), and then a check can be made to see whether these activities fall within poor weather periods.

When should inspections be conducted?

Again, activity coding schemes can come to the scheduler's aid. A code field may be created to indicate which inspections are needed for a particular activity. Another approach to identifying major inspections and other milestones is to use activities that have zero duration. These activities may be selected according to zero duration to obtain a list of milestones. If the schedule uses the Arrow Diagram Method, then a further selection criteria may be necessary to eliminate dummy activities. The scheduler may sort on activities with zero durations that do not have the activity description "Dummy."

What should the contractor be working on this week?

The answer to this question really illustrates the power of many project scheduling systems to provide useful information to the construction team. To obtain this information, the scheduler would run a report that lists all activities that have started, but are not yet complete, and those activities that are scheduled to start within the week. This report may be printed in tabular form or the more widely used bar chart. The scheduler may also qualify the list by selecting activities according to activity codes. One example might be a listing of all mechanical activities that are to take place this week. This data can provide useful information to the construction team.

There are two categories of those activities that are scheduled to start; activities that "may start" and activities that "must start." Those activities that "may start" are the activities whose early dates fall within the week's period. The "must start" activities are those whose late start dates fall within the particular week's period. Unless these "must start" activities begin within that week, the project will fall behind schedule. Activity completion may also be monitored by using the early and late finish dates to determine the "may finish" and "must finish" activities.

Activity Coding in Scheduling Systems

There is wide variation in the actual implementation of coding in project scheduling systems. This subsection includes a description of the very limited coding features provided by most scheduling software, tips for getting the most out of these features, an explanation of other, more flexible types of coding schemes, and notes about utilizing the same basic set of activity codes on all construction projects.

Almost every scheduling program provides at least the following two activity code fields. In the systems oriented toward the construction industry, these codes are often called the *Responsibility* code and the *Work Area* code. The person who inputs schedule data enters the values of these codes for every activity in the lines of the activity data entry form. For some small projects, the Responsibility code and the Work Area code may be used to effectively manage and control a project. On large projects, however, the use of only two codes will significantly impede the effective categorization and reporting of project data.

While the Responsibility and Work Area codes may be labeled "Responsibility" and "Work Area" on the activity data entry form, these fields may actually contain values for any code that the scheduler desires. If the scheduler wanted to use the Responsibility code field to display values of the Construction Specification Institute (CSI), then a wider variation of information may be obtained. The scheduler may still get the Responsibility code information by searching specification sections that have been subcontracted. The Work Area code field could be used to contain values for the *Activity Type* code. An activity's work area may then be designated by ranges of activity identification numbers, corresponding to the various sections of the project.

Another feature that systems with fixed activity code fields often include is access to characters specific to that code. Specifying characters within an activity code field may be used for codes that have multiple levels of meaning. For example, the Construction Specification Institute (CSI) has three levels of meaning. The first level is the overall category of tasks (e.g., mechanical, electrical, etc.). The second level is the general area within a category (e.g., steam distribution, electrical panels, etc.). Finally, the third level is the specific construction item (e.g., valves, circuit breakers, etc.). To utilize the flexibility of this type of code field, the scheduler specifies both the name of the code field, the code value needed, and the position of the needed code value within the code field.

If an office needs additional coding capacity and the purchase of new scheduling software is not possible, then substituting more sophisticated types of coding in existing Responsibility and Work Area code fields may help. In the scheduling systems that predesignate the labels attached to activity codes, these code field values are not actually defined by the system. In other words, just because one of these code fields has a particular name does not necessarily mean it must be used in that way.

Although predesignated activity code fields, such as Responsibility and Work Area, may be defined in various ways, efficient and easily understandable activity coding on larger projects requires that schedulers develop their own set of activity code fields and dictionaries of their values.

Typically, there are two ways that scheduling systems provide user-customized activity codes. The first is to allow the user to define a set number of code fields. Often, these code fields may be of different lengths. For example, a Weather Sensitive code field may be only one character long (for the value "y" for yes) while the Activity Type code field may be four characters in length. The limitation of this type of coding is that there is often a fixed total length for all activity codes. Fortunately, the systems that provide this type of activity coding provide enough space to cover an extensive set of codes. The total coding scheme length limitation almost never causes problems, even on large construction projects.

The second type of flexible activity coding allows the scheduler complete freedom to create an unlimited number of code fields. Often, the capability to create an unlimited number of additional codes fields is based upon the underlying software of the schedule program. If the system developed was based upon one of the many popular database management programs, it should have the capability for unlimited activity coding.

A feature that is often available in systems with sophisticated coding schemes is the *Activity Code Library*. This Activity Code Library allows your office to develop one detailed set of codes fields and utilize that set of codes fields with many different projects. Since typing a large activity coding scheme into a scheduling system may take several hours, the use of one library for many projects is very time efficient. In addition, using one set of codes for all projects will provide consistency among projects and make report generation and analysis easier.

Pitfalls in Using Activity Codes

There are several pitfalls that should be avoided when developing useful activity coding schemes. These pitfalls usually occur when developing initial activity code dictionaries, choosing appropriate values for activity codes, and modifying codes after the start of the project. This section will explain each of these items by providing some examples from real construction projects.

To develop a useful activity coding scheme, the types of information needed to monitor or control construction progress, verify schedule accuracy, and communicate with project stakeholders must be considered. There are three factors often overlooked in developing a useful list. The first factor is that activity codes should be easily understood. For example, if it is decided that the Responsibility code field needs to be used, then the letter "P," to refer to prime contractor activities, and the letter "O," to refer to owner activities, might be used. However, using one character codes will, in many cases, cause more typographical errors and more time spent determining a code's value definition from the Activity Coding Scheme Dictionary.

If possible, code values should be selected based on reasonable abbreviations, not letters or numbers. Table 4.8 illustrates a small portion the values used in a very poor activity code field from a real construction project. The activity code chosen for this example was called the "Sort code" in this project. The intent of the Sort code

Table 4.8. A poor subarea code value definition.

CODE VALUE	DEFINITION
AA	Partitions
AD	Drywall
AF	Firewall
AM	Architectural — Misc.
AP	Precast
AW	Windows/Window Walls
CC	Concrete
CE	Earthwork
CF	Concrete Floors
CMU	CMU Walls
CS	Storm Drains/Culverts
CT	Cooling Tower
CW	Dampproofing
DEMO	Demolition
DW	Domestic Water
EC	Conduit and Cable Tray
ED	Duct Bank
EE	Electrical Equipment
EF	Electrical Fixtures
EG	Underground Electrical
EL	Lighting
ELEV	Elevators
ELP	Parking Lot Lighting

was to allow the scheduler to identify subparts of the project. The first problem with this code field is that the name of the code field, "Sort," is a generic capability of all activity code fields and is not at all descriptive of the contents of the field.

Looking over this list, it might be expected that the items are listed by logical abbreviations. Unfortunately, since each person abbreviates differently, trying to anticipate the code for a particular category often does not work. If, for example, a user tried to think of what the code for dampproofing should be, he would probably not think of the code value actually used, "CW." In another example, a user may try to guess at what code a cooling tower should fall under. They may consider the mechanical items that seem to start with the letter "M." The actual code used, however, is "CT." Using inconsistent codes will force the user to refer to an activity coding dictionary every time they want to do any in-depth report. Consistent codes are essential to the rapid development of ad hoc reports.

The second activity coding problem in the example construction project is that several different codes refer to exactly the same information. If this situation occurs, the user may not be able to determine which of these codes actually refers to the specific data that the user wants to select or sort upon. In this construction, project code fields called Sort, Responsibility, and Levels all contain a value to denote testing activities. During the analysis of this schedule, the reviewers were forced to complete several sorts to check that all possible testing activities were reviewed. In addition to wasting a lot of time checking several codes for the same data, inconsistent coding undermines confidence in the accuracy of the network.

An independent designation of categories for activity codes is critical for large projects. If a project spans several years, the scheme will be difficult to maintain and the persons who developed the initial coding scheme may not be able to explain why certain codes were originally put into the schedule.

Finally, when using codes that relate to specification sections or building systems, schedulers often do not provide sufficient levels of detail for each activity. The depth of the Activity Coding Dictionary is very important for very large projects. A deep material code such as the Construction Specification Index (CSI) will, for example, allow the scheduler to differentiate between structural steel and steel pan forms for concrete slabs. A deep systems code such as the

Building Systems Index (BSI) will, for example, allow the scheduler to differentiate between windows used for exterior closure and casefronts used to separate office spaces. While detailed coding of all of the activities in the schedule appears to be wasted effort, the schedule data can only be turned into effective project information by clearly differentiating between various types of activities. On large projects, the depth of these types of hierarchical codes will determine, to a large extent, the depth of the project monitoring and control tools available to the scheduler.

The final problem that may be encountered when utilizing a complex coding scheme is the need to add new codes after the project has begun. To accomplish this, the user will have to add the new codes to each version of the schedule, and also manually add all of the data into each activity. Often, the need for more detailed analysis occurs when the construction office has a project that appears to be rather straightforward, but turns out to be quite complicated.

Activity coding is a critical element of an effective construction schedule. The coding scheme built into a schedule determines the speed with which reports can be produced and the depth to which schedule analysis may be performed. Since there is a limited amount of time for schedule analysis, activity coding essentially determines the level of analysis, and therefore the degree to which the schedule will be used to manage the job. If a robust coding scheme is not developed at the beginning of a project, then the user can count on spending a significant amount of their time trying to figure out how to get around poor coding and how to "hot wire" new coding into the schedule. On a large project, a scheduler could easily waste four hours a week over a period of several months trying to get information out of a scheduling system that uses a bad activity coding scheme.

MILESTONES AND TARGET DATES

Fixed dates, also known as "plugged dates," may be utilized in many project scheduling systems to add realism to the construction model being created. Some examples of these dates are the contract completion date, the factory delivery dates, and any intermediate notice to proceed based on phased work. These examples will be reviewed, using the piping project schedule presented in Chapter 2, to show how the scheduler might utilize a project scheduling system to model real world constraints.

The first thing to determine when attempting to "plug" predetermined dates into a project scheduling system is to consider the effect of the constraint on the project. As an example, consider the contract completion date. If the project must be finished no later than the contract completion date, then you would want to make sure that, if the schedule slipped past the contract completion date, schedule reports would clearly indicate which activities were causing the delay. Plugged "finish no later than" dates may or may not effect the schedule's calculation date. If the schedule shows completion prior to or on the project finish date, there is no problem, as the contractor has the option of completing the project anytime within the contract period. However, if the schedule extends past this date, the float of the critical path will appear as a negative value. If this condition occurs, all parties to the construction contract should be alerted as soon as possible.

Plugged dates are often used for factory delivery dates, to provide information about what is the latest date that equipment can be delivered and not delay the project. This type of constraint may be referred to as a "finish no later than" constraint, because the equipment delivery may be early, but it cannot finish later than a given date. This type of constraint may be particularly important when a contractor plans on including a large piece of equipment within a room with limited access.

An intermediate Notice to Proceed is the third example of a constraint. Information about when the contractor may start an activity is referred to as a "start no earlier than" constraint because the activity may start no earlier than the Notice to Proceed.

Table 4.9 shows the eight types of dates which may be plugged into a schedule. Not all of these dates may be available in a particular project scheduling system. These dates represent three different levels of schedule constraint which can be applied. Each of these levels provides greater control over the schedule than the previous level. The minimum control available is the "target" date. These plug dates do not effect the schedule but only provide a reference for comparison. A user may control the schedule at an intermediate level by forcing the use of a plug date if the project scheduling

Table 4.9. Types of plugged dates.

MILESTONE	EFFECT ON SCHEDULE CALCULATIONS
target start	This date does not affect the early or late start date, but may be shown in reports to allow user comparisons.
target finish	This date does not affect the early or late finish date, but may be shown in reports to allow user comparisons.
start no earlier than	If the scheduled early start date is prior to plug date, then the plug date replaces the early start date.
finish no earlier than	If the scheduled early finish date is prior to the plug date, then the plug date replaces the early finish date.
start no later than	If the scheduled late start date is past the plug date, then the plug date replaces the late start date.
finish no later than	If the scheduled late finish date is past the plug date, then the plug date replaces the late finish date.
start on	This date replaces both the calculated early and late start dates.
finish on	This date replaces both the calculated early and late finish dates.

system calculates a date which does not meet the necessary conditions. The intermediate level of control is provided by the "no earlier than" and "no later than" dates.

If the user wants to require that an event occur on a certain date regardless of the calculated dates, then the third level of schedule constraint, the "start on" and "finish on" dates, are available. This is the maximum control that the user may exert on the network. Caution should be exercised when utilizing this constraint, since the network logic may be ignored if there is a potential conflict. Given the correct circumstances, this may force an activity to be scheduled to complete prior to its calculated start date. When controlling the schedule with this constraint, the user should also be concerned with the potential disruption to succeeding activities.

When utilizing any of these scheduling constraints, it is also important to make sure that the plug date is a work day. Although some project scheduling systems may allow the user to enter a nonworkday date, this date will not be meaningful to the people who have to use the report. The credibility of the network would substantially decrease if, for example, a particular phase of construction was scheduled to start on December 25th.

Since the use of the "no earlier than," "no later than," "start on," and "finish on" dates will effect the results obtained by the project scheduling system, these plug dates should be used carefully. To create the desired effect on the schedule calculation, it is often necessary to use these dates on a trial and error basis. One of the reasons is that some project scheduling systems may not follow the definitions provided in Table 4.9. If the project team wishes to utilize these dates, all parties should understand their effects on the schedule.

Unexpected results may also occur if more than one plugged date is used in a single path of activities through the network. Using multiple plugged dates often results in a single path of activities having different values of float, due to the "artificial" calculation put on the schedule by these plugged dates.

One date that should typically be plugged into every schedule, however, is the contract completion date. The use of plug dates in the example piping project allows this delay to appear as negative float. For example, if the schedule report had been run with the original completion date of 29 November 1989 as the "finish no later than" date, the result may appear as shown in Table 4.10. The use of these plug dates can therefore be a very effective project management tool.

DEFAULT COMPLETION CALCULATIONS

Although the dates that an activity begins (and ends) should always be entered into the program, the exact date is not always known by the person updating the network. To provide for this situation, many programs allow progress to be defined by entering only the remaining or expended activity duration. However, taking this shortcut is not recommended, since systems differ widely in the method of calculating the schedule, if the actual dates are not provided. This section will illustrate the different ways that some systems may calculate activity completion dates, if actual start dates are not entered for in-progress activities.

There are two situations that could arise if a remaining or expended duration is reported without entering the actual start date of an activity. While the first two examples are straightforward, the third situation reflects (from the authors' perspective) an incorrect approach to scheduling philosophy.

Table 4.10. Updated schedule using a "plugged" completion date.

ACTIVITY/ SUCCESSORS	DESCRIPTION	ORIGINAL DURATION	REMAINING DURATION	EARLY START/FINISH	LATE START/FINISH	FLOAT
1/ 2, 3	Start Job	1	0	2 Oct 89 A	2 Oct 89 A	
2/ 10	Relocate Electric	6	3	9 Oct 89 A 6 Nov 89	20 Nov 89	10
3/ 4	Excavate	3	0	5 Oct 89 A	9 Oct 89 A	
4/ 5, 6	Install Pipe Section One	10	0	12 Oct 89 A	25 Oct 89 A	
5/ 7	Backfill Section One	5	0	26 Oct 89 A	1 Nov 89 A	
6/ 7, 8	Install Pipe Section Two	12	6	26 Oct 89 A 9 Nov 89	6 Nov 89 7 Nov 89	−3
7/ 9	Backfill Section Two	8	8	10 Nov 89 21 Nov 89	16 Nov 89 14 Nov 89	−3
8/ 9, 10	Test Pipe Sections	3	3	10 Nov 89 14 Nov 89	16 Nov 89 17 Nov 89	2
9/ 12	Grade & Sod	7	7	22 Nov 89 1 Dec 89	28 Nov 89 21 Nov 89	−3
10/ 11	Install Manhole	3	3	15 Nov 89 17 Nov 89	24 Nov 89 27 Nov 89	4
11/ 12	Test Electric	2	2	20 Nov 89 21 Nov 89	28 Nov 89 29 Nov 89	4
12/	Inspect	1	1	4 Dec 89 4 Dec 89	29 Nov 89*	−3

The first situation occurs when the data date is the same date as an activity's early start date. The program assigns the data date as the actual start date and then calculates the early finish date as the actual start date plus the remaining duration. Figure 4.1 provides an example of this situation.

While the first example seems to be what one might expect a program to do, there are other factors to consider prior to using this default feature provided by some scheduling systems. One of the most important reasons for utilizing a construction network is to communicate about both the current situation and the historical record to those who may need to review the project later. The system that uses the default calculations masks the actual start by setting the actual start date, in reports, as equal to the data date. Scheduling systems that do not provide some type of identification for activities that utilize default information should be thoroughly investigated prior to use by a construction office.

In the second and third examples of using default values for early start dates, the actual start date of an activity precedes the data date. Each example reflects the application of a different scheduling algorithm, depending on the project scheduling system being used. In

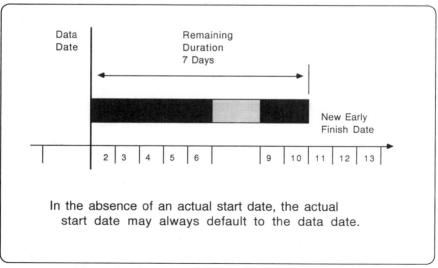

Figure 4.1. Data date defaults to the actual start date.

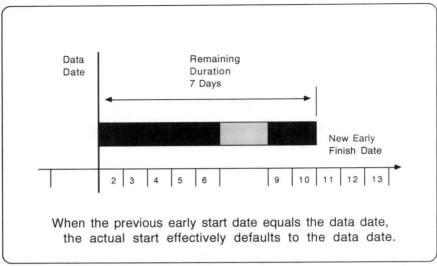

When the previous early start date equals the data date,
the actual start effectively defaults to the data date.

Figure 4.2. Defaults when the early start equals the data date.

the second example, the default actual start date is set equal to the data date, and (as in the first example) the early finish is the sum of the default date and the remaining duration. Figure 4.2 shows the result of this type of calculation.

The third default scheduling algorithm will calculate a different early finish date for the activity. This algorithm sets the actual start to the activity's previously calculated early start date. The early finish is then the sum of the activity's previous early start date and the remaining duration. As shown by Figure 4.3, the early finish date for this activity will be earlier than in the second example. The activity will finish early by the number of days difference between the previously calculated early start and the data date. If this difference is larger than the remaining duration entered by the user, some programs may indicate that the activity has been completed. Figure 4.3 also graphically illustrates this third scheduling algorithm.

In the authors' opinion, the default calculation illustrated in this third scenario is incorrect, because it assumes that progress is ongoing when, in fact, there may have been no progress since the previous period. Fortunately, most scheduling systems do not follow the third type of default calculation, but calculate default completion dates based on the data date. Although most systems do not

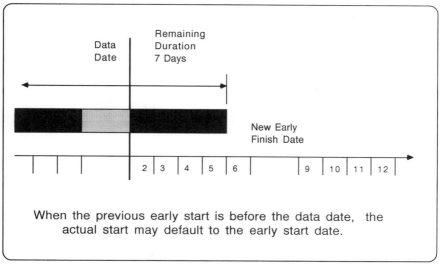

When the previous early start is before the data date, the actual start may default to the early start date.

Figure 4.3. Defaults when the early start is prior to the data date.

incorporate this third type of calculation, the schedule practitioner should be on the watch for difficulties arising from the use of default activity progress calculations.

Default dates should not be used unless sufficient time is available for an analysis of potential conflicts that might occur. If a construction office discovers that the program used inserts default dates into the schedule, then the office needs to be careful to insure that any activities that are going to show progress have an Actual Start Date and Remaining Duration. Requiring that an actual start date (even if the date is an estimate) is always entered for every in-progress activity is the proper way to post progress to an activity. Insuring that an actual start date is entered will also prove valuable if the project must be reconstructed for later claims.

OUT-OF-SEQUENCE PROGRESS CALCULATIONS

It is expected that the critical path models developed at the beginning of a project will change as the project team evaluates the most efficient means of completing the project. One example of this type of change occurs when a schedule calls for one activity to precede another activity, whereas on the construction site both activities are underway. This situation is called "out-of-sequence" progress.

Project scheduling systems generally allow one of three ways to schedule a network with out-of-sequence progress. The first method is not to allow out-of-sequence progress at all. That is, if the network contains out-of-sequence progress, then the software will provide an error message identifying those activities that are out-of-sequence and will not calculate the schedule. This approach to out-of-sequence progress will require the scheduler to change the logic of the schedule to alleviate the out-of-sequence progress, prior to allowing a recalculation of the network.

The second and third methods used by scheduling software to handle out-of-sequence progress are not the only methods that may be used, but do represent the most widely used methods in the construction industry today. These two methods are called the Logical Calculation Method (LCM) and the Progress Calculation Method (PCM). The differences between these two methods will be illustrated by adding out-of-sequence progress to the piping project example presented in Table 3.3. If we change activity number 7, "Backfill Section Two," in Table 3.3 to show an actual start date of October 31, 1989, and a remaining duration of seven days, then we have created an out-of-sequence situation, because activity 6, "Install Pipe Section Two," has not been completed.

The difficulty when working with out-of-sequence progress is that the LCM and PCM can calculate different project completion dates. After adding the out-of-sequence activity 7 to the piping project, and obtaining a LCM and PCM schedule calculation, two schedule reports were printed. These reports are shown in Tables 4.11 and 4.12. Using LCM, as shown in Table 4.11, activity 12, "Inspect," is completed on December 1, 1989. Under PCM, shown in Table 4.12, the project, and activity 12, complete on November 27, 1989.

The difference in project completion dates between out-of-sequence progress calculated by LCM and PCM may cause confusion and mistrust in schedule data by management and schedule users. The scheduler should know, therefore, how these methods of calculation operate.

To calculate the schedule for out-of-sequence progress, the Logical Calculation Method (LCM) performs three actions, as illustrated by Figure 4.4. The first action of the LCM calculates the early finish

Table 4.11. Out-of-sequence schedule report using LCM.

ACTIVITY/SUCCESSORS	DESCRIPTION	ORIGINAL DURATION	REMAINING DURATION	EARLY START/FINISH	LATE START/FINISH	FLOAT
1/ 2, 3	Start Job	1	0	2 Oct 89 A	2 Oct 89 A	
2/ 10	Relocate Electric	6	3	9 Oct 89 A / 6 Nov 89	9 Oct 89 A / 22 Nov 89	12
3/ 4	Excavate	3	0	5 Oct 89 A	9 Oct 89 A	
4/ 5, 6	Install Pipe Section One	10	0	12 Oct 89 A	25 Oct 89 A	
5/ 7	Backfill Section One	5	0	26 Oct 89 A	1 Nov 89 A	
6/ 7, 8	Install Pipe Section Two	12	6	26 Oct 89 A / 9 Nov 89	9 Nov 89	0
7/ 9	Backfill Section Two	8	7	31 Oct 89 A / 20 Nov 89	20 Nov 89	0
8/ 9, 10	Test Pipe Sections	3	3	10 Nov 89 / 14 Nov 89	16 Nov 89 / 20 Nov 89	4
9/ 12	Grade & Sod	7	7	21 Nov 89 / 30 Nov 89	21 Nov 89 / 30 Nov 89	0
10/ 11	Install Manhole	3	3	15 Nov 89 / 17 Nov 89	24 Nov 89 / 28 Nov 89	6
11/ 12	Test Electric	2	2	20 Nov 89 / 21 Nov 89	29 Nov 89 / 30 Nov 89	6
12/	Inspect	1	1	1 Dec 89 / 1 Dec 89	1 Dec 89 / 1 Dec 89	0

Table 4.12. Out-of-sequence schedule report using PCM.

ACTIVITY/ SUCCESSORS	DESCRIPTION	ORIGINAL DURATION	REMAINING DURATION	EARLY START/FINISH	LATE START/FINISH	FLOAT
1/ 2, 3	Start Job	1	0	2 Oct 89 A	2 Oct 89 A	
2/ 10	Relocate Electric	6	3	9 Oct 89 A / 6 Nov 89	16 Nov 89	8
3/ 4	Excavate	3	0	5 Oct 89 A	9 Oct 89 A	
4/ 5, 6	Install Pipe Section One	10	0	12 Oct 89 A	25 Oct 89 A	
5/ 7	Backfill Section One	5	0	26 Oct 89 A	1 Nov 89 A	
6/ 7, 8	Install Pipe Section Two	12	6	26 Oct 89 A / 9 Nov 89	9 Nov 89	0
7/ 9	Backfill Section Two	8	7	31 Oct 89 A / 10 Nov 89	14 Nov 89	2
8/ 9, 10	Test Pipe Sections	3	3	10 Nov 89 / 14 Nov 89	10 Nov 89 / 14 Nov 89	0
9/ 12	Grade & Sod	7	7	15 Nov 89 / 24 Nov 89	15 Nov 89 / 24 Nov 89	0
10/ 11	Install Manhole	3	3	15 Nov 89 / 17 Nov 89	17 Nov 89 / 21 Nov 89	2
11/ 12	Test Electric	2	2	20 Nov 89 / 21 Nov 89	22 Nov 89 / 24 Nov 89	2
12/	Inspect	1	1	27 Nov 89 / 27 Nov 89	27 Nov 89 / 27 Nov 89	0

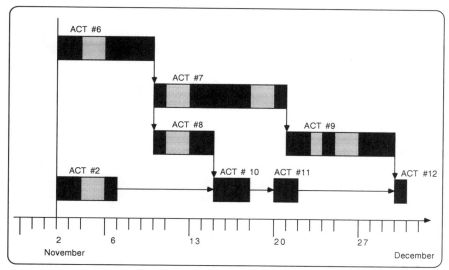

Figure 4.4. Logical calculation method (LCM).

of activity number 6, by adding the remaining duration of activity 6 (seven days) to the data date of November 2, 1989. This provides an early finish date for activity 6 of November 9, 1989.

The second action of the LCM is to override the actual start date for activity 7 and, for the purposes of schedule calculation, base the start date for the activity 7 to be the early finish of activity 6. Since the early finish date for activity 6 is November 9, 1989, the early start for activity 7 is the next day, November 10, 1989.

The important feature of LCM is that the logic between the two activities is retained, since the finish of activity 6 is the basis for calculating the start of activity 7. This, as will be shown, is quite different from the PCM analysis.

The last step of the LCM calculates the early finish date for activity 7 as the sum of the temporary start date, November 10, 1989, and the remaining duration of activity 7, seven days. Therefore, the early finish of activity 7 will be November 20, 1989.

Other activities in the network are calculated based on the traditional CPM method. Following these other activities in the network, shown in Figure 4.4, the project should complete on December 1, 1989.

One additional feature of LCM is that the scheduling software will not allow activity 7 to complete prior to activity 6. If this condition occurs during updating, the schedule will not calculate, but will instead print an error message.

The Progress Calculation Method (PCM), shown in Figure 4.5, disregards the relationship between the out-of-sequence activity and the rest of the schedule. Notice that the early finish of activity 7 is obtained by adding the remaining duration of this out-of-sequence activity, seven days, to the data date. Using PCM, the early finish of activity 7 is November 10, 1989. Under the LCM method, the early finish of activity 7 was November 20, 1989.

In PCM, start and finish dates for other activities are calculated independently of the out-of-sequence activity. As shown in Figure 4.5, the project completion date is November 27, 1989.

If out-of-sequence progress is allowed, the scheduler should review the way in which the construction team's scheduling software calculates out-of-sequence activities. A conservative approach in determining the completion of a particular activity on the schedule is recommended.

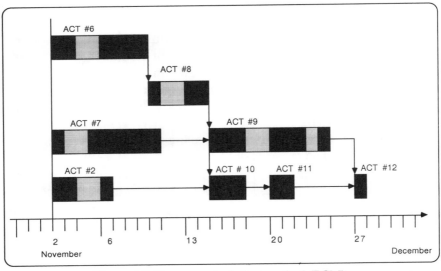

Figure 4.5. Progress calculation method (PCM).

Using a conservative approach, LCM should be used to schedule out-of-sequence activities. LCM is more conservative for two reasons. First, because most project scheduling systems using LCM do not allow out-of-sequence activities completed prior to their succeeding activities. The second is because LCM will always leave less float on the critical path than PCM. The largest that the float in the PCM method will be is the difference between the early finish of the preceding activity and the data date.

Out-of-sequence progress is a very controversial issue in scheduling today. The controversy arises from differences in scheduling philosophies. At one end of the spectrum are those who feel that a network should always reflect the exact method of actual construction. These individuals would require that network logic be changed for all out-of-sequence activities. At the other end of the spectrum are those who feel that construction sequence changes do not need to be reflected in a network that rarely even approximates the construction process. These persons feel that the logic for out-of-sequence activities never needs to be changed. The question of how to handle out-of-sequence progress needs to be based on an analysis of the appropriate level of network accuracy required for payment and progress control.

Unless out-of-sequence progress extends beyond a single schedule update period, the logic of out-of-sequence progress, in the authors' opinion, need not be revised. Out-of-sequence progress is typically the result of changes in the sequence of various work crews through the construction project. In most cases, these activities will be completed prior to the next update. The effort to break up out-of-sequence activities into smaller segments and add logic relationships for these activities is much better spent in more effective use of existing data and planning for major upcoming changes to the construction plan.

On the other hand, out-of-sequence progress that extends beyond a single update period should be quickly modified to reflect the actual construction conditions. Since project monitoring is tied directly to schedule activities, out-of-sequence progress that extends beyond the payment period will not reflect the actual progress. Unless these activities are changed, there will not be a sound basis for determining project status in future updates.

ADDING COST DATA TO ACTIVITIES

There are at least two different approaches to assigning cost information to activities: a construction contractor's perspective and the owner's perspective. These two approaches are very different, although most project scheduling systems liberally mix their terminology. This section will introduce and define a consistent terminology that may be used to assist the construction team in communicating about cost information, and to isolate problems that may occur as a result of misinterpretations.

From the contractor's point of view, there are three categories of cost associated with any one activity on a fixed-priced contract. These categories reflect the interactive process that most contractors utilize to arrive at project costs. The first category is an "estimated cost" to complete an activity. The estimated cost may actually be a rough breakdown from a building system, such as an air conditioning system, which was determined as a lump sum cost in the contractor's bid. The "budgeted cost" is what the contractor feels the activity may actually cost. Finally, the "actual cost" is what the contractor actually spends in the process of construction.

From an owner's perspective on a fixed-priced contract, "activity cost" refers to the fixed amount that the owner has agreed to pay the contractor in return for completing the work described by an activity. This cost is generally assumed to be spread evenly over each day of an activity. This type of activity cost allocation is called *time-based.*

When the activity cost does not have a constant dollar per day rate, then the contractor has two alternatives for obtaining financial compensation. The first type of cost allocation, *fiscal completion,* is typically used when the contractor has a large dollar investment to make prior to actual work beginning. The primary use of fiscal completion is to pay the contractor for materials on-site.

The other type of cost allocation may occur when the contractor actually completes most of the work at the beginning of an activity. This type of cost allocation is called *physical completion.* One example of this type of activity is concrete placement, as most of the work is completed shortly after the concrete is placed inside the forms.

Figure 4.6 shows the dollar per day allocation of the time-based, fiscal completion, and physical completion types of cost.

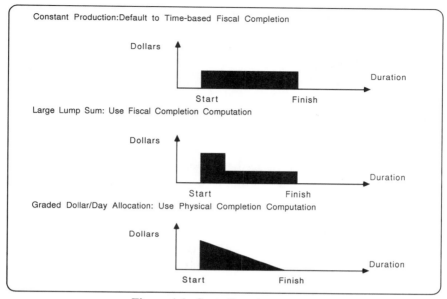

Figure 4.6. Cost allocation curves.

Because of the complexity in allocating costs to an activity, the assignment of costs to activities is highly dependent on the interpretation of these complexities in the particular project scheduling system being used. Some programs allow for the entering of the activity cost with the activity identification and logical relationship descriptions, while others require that some form of resource or cost accounts be set up to monitor costs more closely.

While a variety of approaches to cost may be of great benefit to the contractor, the construction office staff who regularly use the project scheduling system must become familiar with the features that meet the owner's requirements and should carefully review the contractor's use of these cost fields.

Though it is generally assumed that an activity should be billed to the owner in accordance with the time-based completion of the activity, many project scheduling systems also recognize the other two methods of reporting cost completion of an activity. Since these programs are, however, oriented toward the contractor's monitoring of estimated, budgeted, and actual cost, reporting cost is another area that the project team should agree upon prior to the submission of the initial schedule.

Several project scheduling systems calculate the payment due the contractor through a series of three default settings: time-based percent complete, physical percent complete, and fiscal completion. The initial default value, time-based percent complete, is determined by dividing the expended duration by the original duration. Earned value will be calculated, in this case as the product of the activity cost and time-based percent complete. If percent complete is entered, then some project scheduling systems assume that this data represents the physical completion of the activity. In this case, the time-based percent complete is not calculated and the physical percent complete is used to calculate the earned value.

The final tier of the default cost scheme would be entering an actual dollar amount to represent the payment due the contractor for the earned value of work in place. This is referred to as fiscal completion. Table 4.13 illustrates the way in which this hierarchy

Table 4.13. Earned value hierarchy.

TIME-BASED PERCENT COMPLETE:

Example Activity:	#2, Relocate Electric
Original Duration:	6 Days
Remaining Duration:	3 Days
Time-Based Completion:	(Days Expended / Original Duration) × (100%)
	(3 / 6) × (100%) = 50%
Earned Value:	(Activity Cost) × (Time-Based Completion)
	$4,200 × 50% = $2,100

PHYSICAL PERCENT COMPLETE:

Example Activity:	#6, Install Pipe Section Two
Time-Based Completion:	(6 / 12) × 100% = 50%
Physical Completion:	70%
Earned Value:	(Activity Cost) × (Physical Completion)
	$14,400 × 70% = $10,080

FISCAL COMPLETION:

Example Activity:	#10, Install Manhole
Time-Based Completion:	0%
Material Delivery:	$1,000
Earned Value:	$1,000

Table 4.14. Posted cost data.

ACTIVITY NUMBER	DESCRIPTION	ACTIVITY COST	ORIGINAL DURATION	REMAINING DURATION	PHYSICAL-PERCENT COMPLETE	EARNED VALUE
1	Start Job	0	1	0		$ 0
2	Relocate Electric	4,200	6	3		$ 2,100
3	Excavate	3,000	3	0		$ 3,000
4	Install Pipe Section One	12,000	10	0		$12,000
5	Backfill Section One	3,500	5	0		$ 3,500
6	Install Pipe Section Two	14,400	12	6	70	$10,080
7	Backfill Section Two	5,600	8	6		$ 1,400
8	Test Pipe Sections	1,500	3	3		
9	Grade & Sod	2,100	7	7		
10	Install Manhole	3,000	3	3		$ 1,000
11	Test Electric	6,000	2	2		
12	Inspect	0	1	1		
	Total	$55,300			60%	$33,080

might work on several activities in the example pipe project. Table 4.14 shows the cost progress posted along with the latest update of the example pipe schedule.

The details of performing cost analysis depends, to a great extent, on the particular program being used. While the hierarchy presented for determining a contractor's payment is the most common among the project scheduling systems surveyed, there are many other approaches to determining earned value. Some of these other approaches require the user to provide completely separate cost and time data without any default values. The comprehensive methods provide the user with multiple cost accounts per project, data fields for materials on-site, data fields for changes in the original cost of an activity due to contract modification, and also allow the user to manipulate unit cost and activity quantities. Depending on the needs of the construction office, some of these alternatives may be very important features. These options are not as important, however, as the need for an agreement between members of the construction team on the way in which time-based, physical, and fiscal completion methods will be used during the term of the contract.

Chapter 5

Scheduling Implementation Issues

INTRODUCTION

Learning how to use a scheduling system efficiently is only one aspect of effective implementation of a scheduling system. The other aspects of effective scheduling that will be discussed in this chapter are selecting scheduling software, specifying construction scheduling, schedule data exchange, integration of scheduling systems with other data systems, and using schedules for construction claims analysis. The first topic is selecting the best software for the job. Through a discussion of software selection, the reader can develop a detailed list of features that should be considered when purchasing scheduling software. The software selection section will also show how scheduling systems effect the construction office. The second topic is how to specify construction schedules. The third issue is data exchange between scheduling systems, so that schedule data may be shared among the members of the construction team. A discussion of the potential for integrating scheduling data with other types of automated systems for the construction office is the next topic. Finally, effective use of schedules to justify time extensions due to changes and claims will also be addressed.

SELECTING A SCHEDULING SYSTEM

One of the most important decisions that will be made in scheduling is the choice of software. Unfortunately, this decision is frequently underemphasized. Typically, the selection of software is based on published surveys or recommendations by other users. Both of these selection methods have flaws that could keep these scheduling methods from being used effectively, or from ever using them in the first place.[1]

While software surveys published in computer magazines provide an overall discussion of the capabilities of a large number of products, the basis for ranking systems presented in these articles may not be appropriate for all uses of scheduling systems. Since scheduling software is generally updated every six to twelve months, these reports are often outdated. In addition, these reviews frequently rely on project minutia to determine the quality of the software. For example, multicolor, three-dimensional bar charts may show that one system provides 24 characters for an activity description, and another system provides 25. While this type of data makes very nice graphics, it seldom assists in selecting software. Faced with inadequate project reviews, the person or team evaluating scheduling programs often turns to reviews by other users.

Discussions with other users of scheduling systems may be very helpful. However, these users may not have a workload that directly corresponds to that of the inquiring office. The availability of computers, experience of the office staff, the type of contract documents that govern scheduling systems, and other critical areas for selecting software, may be different from that of the inquiring office.

Hundreds of organizations spend from six to twelve months and tens of thousands of dollars yearly selecting a project scheduling system. The selection procedure described below will enable schedulers to reduce the time and cost of selecting a system, and thereby increasing the time that is available to use the system efficiently. A reduction in selection cost and time are obtained by using the format of the selection guide, rather than traditional selection methods. An improvement in scheduling efficiency will occur if, during the selection process, ways that the scheduling system will be used by the construction office can be anticipated.

The selection method given below is based on several sets of rules. These rules first gather information about the construction office's size of projects, types of projects, and what kind of business the

---

[1]East, E. William. Approaches to selecting project management systems. *Proceedings of the 5th Computing in Civil Engineering Conference.* ASCE, March 1988. pp. 52–60.

office is engaged in. Based on this data, a list of scheduling software features that will support the office is identified. After answering other questions regarding contracts, computer experience, and computer hardware, a list of features to consider when implementing the system that matches the list of features in the office will be developed. This selection method was designed to be flexible enough for application to almost any project type, because the user can make minor modifications to the rules, depending upon local conditions.[2]

The first assumption to be made in the selection method is that scheduling software, or as it is sometimes referred to, project management software, should be chosen only if the needs of the office will be met. While this should be an obvious assumption, only limited consideration is usually given to this essential criteria. The key areas that the office needs to consider are the projects to be scheduled and the type of business that the office does.

To assist in the explanation of the selection method, an example office will be used. The example office is a small-to-medium size construction firm with limited experience in microcomputer-based scheduling. The office has just received an award for a $10,000,000 contract, and has a $30,000,000 contract that requires monthly CPM updates to be used as a justification for payment. The office has several microcomputers that are used by the office clerical staff, but the technical staff has not used a microcomputer before. This construction office will be examined based on the criteria in the selection guide to highlight the features that it should consider when purchasing a scheduling system.

The approach described in this section, while tailored to the specialized field of construction scheduling, may be applied to many other types of businesses as well. The selection method outlined is flexible because an effort has been made to describe the assumptions underlying the conclusions. The non-construction industry reader who uses this method can modify the answers and conclusions based on assumptions that meet their particular needs.

---

[2]East, E. William. Knowledge-based approach to project scheduling system selection. *Journal of Computing in Civil Engineering*, ASCE. Vol. 2, No. 4, Oct 1988. pp. 307–328.

SOFTWARE SELECTION GUIDE

The first, and most critical, area in selecting a system is evaluating the size and type of construction projects at an office. The size of the office work load will determine the relative need for quick access to specific information for a given project. For example, if a construction management office had thirty $1,000,000 projects that it needed to schedule, then rapid access to individual project data would be very important. On the other hand, if the office were to automate only one $500,000 project, then quick data retrieval would not be as critical, since project information is readily available.

Identification of the type of construction office is important, in order to evaluate the office's need for cost control. A construction contractor, for example, must be able to closely monitor budgeted costs, estimated costs, and expected payments. A construction owner, on the other hand, typically only needs the cost data required to monitor expected payments.

Evaluating the Project Work Load

The size of an office work load that effects scheduling selection may be approximated by the total number of activities for the largest project and for all projects to be scheduled. A rule-of-thumb of 200 activities per million project dollars may be used for midrise apartment or office buildings. As the type of building changes, the rule-of-thumb should also be revised appropriately. In addition, a portion of those projects that currently use manual critical path analysis should be included, since they may eventually be analyzed with the microcomputer system.

To determine the number of activities per project, and for the total of all projects, it will be necessary to complete Table 5.1. The first two items in the table are "Number of Projects to be Scheduled" and "Size of Projects." For the example office, there are two projects to be scheduled and the total cost of the projects is $40,000,000. The third item in the table, "Activities per Project," is a variable item that may be changed based on the complexity and

Table 5.1. Size of schedules worksheet.

1. Number of Projects to be Scheduled	=	2
a. Project one = $10,000,000		
b. Project two = $30,000,000		
2. Total Project Cost (in $1,000,000)	=	40
3. Activities per Million (default)	=	200
4. Minimum Activities per Current Project		
a. Project two = $ 30M		
b. Suggested activities = 6000		
c. Safety factor (10%) = 600		
d. Suggest activities per project	=	6600
5. Total Activities for Current Projects		
a. Project One and Two = $ 40M		
b. Suggested activities = 8000		
c. Safety factor (10%) = 800		
d. Total activities for all projects	=	8800

duration of the projects to be scheduled. If it is assumed that the example construction office's projects are both midrise apartment buildings, then 200 activities per million dollars may be used. Determining the minimum number of activities for the largest project is the next step. The larger project in our example is $30,000,000. This figure is multiplied by the same number of activities per million dollars, shown under item three. This multiplication yields the information that the scheduling system should be able to handle a minimum of 6000 activities. Since the number of activities per project is only an estimate, a "safety factor" of an additional 10 percent activity capacity should also be added, yielding a total suggested activity per project of 6,600 activities. The suggested number of activities per project will be checked against the capacity of any scheduling systems that are being considered. This will insure that the system can handle the largest schedule. To complete this first worksheet, the total number of activities for all projects will be estimated. This total number of activities will assist in determining the amount of hard-disk storage that is necessary for the scheduling computer.

Considering Future Project Work Load

The size and type of projects that the office works on may change in the near future. Anticipating changes to the number and type of projects to be scheduled will assist in identifying the system that will be useful for the longest period possible. If, for example, the firm has, in the future, several very large projects requiring a CPM schedule, then increasing the project sizes in the Table 5.1 evaluation should be considered, to insure that the software being considered can handle larger projects. Failing to consider upcoming large projects may require the office to purchase additional software.

The three work load factors that should be evaluated for changes over time are shown in Table 5.2. The first factor to be considered is the possibility of potentially larger projects, as noted in worksheet item one. For the example project office, there is another multimillion dollar project expected in the near future. However, it does not exceed the $30,000,000 project shown in Table 5.1. If, however, there were a larger project, then the new maximum number of activities would have to be recalculated, based on the future project.

The second and third factors that may change the future scheduling needs are the number of projects to be scheduled. If it is anticipated that either more new projects will require scheduling, or that existing types of projects currently being done by the firm will require scheduling, then the total number of activities to be scheduled in the office will need to be revised. Items two and three of Table 5.2 provide spaces to indicate responses to these questions. There are no changes anticipated for the example office.

Table 5.2. Potential future expansion worksheet.

1. Do you anticipate that a project to be scheduled within the next two years could exceed the current largest project? (Yes/No)
   If yes, recalculate the maximum number of activities based for the largest project from Table 5.1.
2. Do you anticipate that the number of projects that require automated scheduling will increase? (Yes/No)
   If yes, recalculate the total number of activities to be scheduled from Table 5.1.
3. Do you anticipate that some of the manual scheduling currently done will be accomplished, in the near future, using scheduling software?
   If yes, recalculate the total number of activities to be scheduled from Table 5.1.

Office Work Load

The office work load has a significant impact on the type of system that is best suited for the office. In this selection criteria, the number of activities for all projects and the type of construction will influence the office work load. There are three assumptions for these rules: the larger the number of activities at an office, the more important the need is to have rapid and flexible access to that information; unit price construction will require unit cost and cost coding features; and contractors will require resource analysis features. It is very important that these assumptions are clearly stated, so that a reviewer of the results of the selection can understand exactly why certain choices have been made in the system feature selection rules. The evaluator or reviewer may, under special circumstances, wish to modify the application of these rules based on local criteria.

Table 5.3 provides a worksheet for the calculation of scheduling features required, based on the project work load of the example office. The first refers to small projects, those under 200 activities. Small projects do not need a large number of sophisticated features for adequate scheduling. The scheduler can review the small project schedule without many computerized analysis tools. A simple CPM or small project, such as the Chapter Three example Spiral Court Apartment project, with repetitive groups of activities, can provide a significant level of analysis capability by using consistent activity identification numbers and a few appropriate activity codes. No sophisticated software analysis features are necessary.

If the largest project to be scheduled contains between 200 and 1000 activities, then the scheduling software selected should allow rapid access to activity data and rapid update of schedule data. The scheduler should also be able to specify criteria for sorting and selecting data based on a per task basis. As a project becomes larger, the scheduler can also select ranges of activities based on activity dates or durations.

As a project moves past the 1000 activity mark, the scheduler will need increased capability to manage the large volume of scheduling data. Particularly necessary are very flexible coding schemes that provide multiple ways to retrieve needed subsets of activities.

Table 5.3. Required software features, based on project size.

1. If the largest project to be scheduled has below 200 activities, then the following scheduling software features should efficiently support your effort:
    a. A system that relies only on a graphical interface for data entry is very appropriate for this range of activities.
    b. The system need only provide one type of data entry screen for creating and updating activities.
    c. The system need only to provide access to activities through entry of activity numbers.
    d. Schedule updates may be created by renaming the entire schedule.
    e. The system need only produce printed reports.
    f. The system need only have two activity codes.
2. If the largest project to be scheduled has between 200 and 1000 activities, then the following scheduling software features should efficiently support your efforts:
    a. All of the items in number 1.
    b. The scheduling system should provide between two and four activity codes of four characters each.
    c. The scheduling system may allow code libraries.
3. If the largest project to be scheduled has over 1000 activities, then the following scheduling software features should efficiently support your efforts:
    a. All items in number 2 above.
    b. The system should provide activity code libraries.
    c. The system may allow the user to define either sets of reports that may be run simultaneously or commands to be executed by internal "batch" or "macro" programs.

Type of Office

The type of construction office generally falls into one of three categories of organizations: owners or representatives, construction management organizations, and contractors. Each organization has priorities that will effect the usefulness of certain system features.

An owner, or his representative, is not typically interested in analyzing resources, because the contractor is usually responsible for resource allocation and productivity. From the contractor's point of view, resource allocation, leveling, and monitoring may be an essential part of any project management automation effort. The needs of a construction management firm often fall between the owner's need for cost control and the contractor's need for resource

Table 5.4. Office type worksheet.

1. Which term most closely indicates the type of work that is accomplished in your office?
   a. Owner or owner's representative
   b. Construction manager
   c. Construction contractor

management. Table 5.4 helps to select the type of office that the scheduling system will be used in.

The type of office implies specific features that should be incorporated into scheduling software to adequately support office managerial needs. The features required by the type of office may not be necessary for small or uncomplicated projects. However, for large and complex projects, the lack of these features could be serious. Table 5.5 provides a list of suggested features based on office type.

Checking Constraints

By using Tables 5.1 through 5.5, it can be determined which specific software features will support the office scheduling needs. These features, however, are not the only items to consider. Many other factors, such as contract restrictions, personnel experience, computer availability, separate office sites, also enter into the process. This portion of the selection process will check to discover which office features can be easily implemented. The worksheets that follow may also provide concrete recommendations about the way the office may need to change in order to efficiently use scheduling software.

Construction Contract Restrictions

The selection of scheduling software also depends on owner placed contractual requirements. There are, typically, three ways that an owner can use contract language in a scheduling specification. The first is to limit the network model to either ADM or PDM, and the second is to specifically require use of a particular scheduling system. The last way that an owner may restrict a construction contract

Table 5.5. Required features based on type of office.

1. If the construction office is that of an owner or owner's representative, then the following scheduling software features would efficiently support the office's needs:
   a. The system should allow fiscal completion to be directly entered for each activity independently from the time-based percent complete of the activity.
   b. The system should allow fiscal completion to be entered as a percentage of the total activity cost independently from the time-based percent complete of the activity.
   c. Without specific cost completion information for an activity, the system may provide a default cost completion figure based on the time-based percent complete of an activity.
2. If the construction office is a construction management office, then the following scheduling software features would efficiently support the office's needs:
   a. All items in number 1.
   b. The system should provide cost coding capabilities.
   c. The system should allow the user to develop cost code libraries that may be used on many projects.
   d. The system should provide resource coding capabilities.
   e. The system should provide resource coding libraries that may be used on many projects.
3. If the construction office is a contractor's office, then the following scheduling software features would efficiently support the office's needs:
   a. All items in number 2.
   b. The system should provide special cost fields representing unit cost items and determine cost completion by the number of units placed to date.
   c. The system should provide cumulative daily resource usage data and charts.
   d. The system should provide resource leveling and constraining algorithms to assist the scheduler in evaluating alternative resource allocations.

is to define the way in which project data may be electronically transferred.

In creating these specifications, an owner should keep in mind that the purpose of the schedule is to improve planning and communication regarding project progress. Restrictive specifications may work against improvements in communication. Specifications may have either direct or indirect methods of calling for specific software. The direct method is to specifically name the software program in the specifications. The indirect method of specifying scheduling software is to indicate a data format exchange methodology that is only applicable for one particular system. Particularly in public agency contracts, scheduling specifications should be checked to see whether proprietary data exchange requirements exists.

Limitations on data transfer through some neutral format is a very appropriate specification provision. By using a neutral format, the construction team can directly input scheduling data, rather than reentering the information into another system. Owners' efforts to develop data exchange formats were started by the Veteran's Administration and, more recently, by the U.S. Army Corps of Engineers, in conjunction with a consortium of scheduling software manufacturers and professional and trade organizations.

Table 5.6 provides a checklist for verifying the limitations on

Table 5.6. Checking contract restrictions.

1. Does the contract specifically require ADM? (If yes, see below)   = _____
   Unless you are already using a system that does not use the Arrow Diagram Method, you should select a program that allows either: only ADM or both ADM and PDM.
2. Does the contract specifically require PDM? (If yes, see below)   = _____
   Unless you are already using a system that does not use the Precedence Diagram Method, you should select a program that allows either: only PDM or both ADM and PDM.
3. Does the contract directly or indirectly require one software system? (If yes, see below)   = _____
   If you are already using scheduling software, you should try to replace this requirement with electronic data exchange in a neutral format. If you are not currently using scheduling, then you should evaluate the specified system to see if it meets your office's needs.
4. Does the contract specify electronic exchange of schedule data? (If yes, see below)   = _____
   You should try to identify which format is being required and determine whether the software that meets your office's needs is able to support that format.
5. Does the contract specifically require plotted network diagrams? (If yes, see below)   = _____
   If plotted diagrams are required, then the software must be capable of producing plots and a plotter and proper cabling should be installed at your office. This capability may cost up to $10,000 over the cost of a full-featured CPM program.

scheduling software that may exist due to contract specifications. It should be verified that all appropriate restrictions have been met prior to purchasing the software.

Personnel Considerations

Failure to effectively implement any type of software is usually the result of a user's dissatisfaction with that software. Therefore, a program that is not too difficult to use, given the time available to learn the program, must be selected. The four items that an office should be evaluated on, prior to selecting the system, are: computer systems experience, available time, staff turnover, and separated sites.

Computer System Experience

The computer experience, as it relates to project management system selection, is a function of three variables: manual network analysis experience, microcomputer experience, and automated project management experience. The level of experience, in both the office and the scheduler, will directly effect the amount of time required to efficiently utilize a project management system. The user who has only worked with manual analysis will take longer to learn the program than the user who has had both microcomputer and manual analysis experience. Personnel who have used automated project scheduling systems, on either micro- or mainframe computers, will take even less time to learn the same project management system, since this user will have a frame of reference from which to approach a new system.

Using these three factors, the time required to learn the scheduling system may be evaluated. Table 5.7 provides a suggested method for determining the time required to learn a system. To use this worksheet, each question needs to be answered, and the points associated with the answer noted. Reference to Tables 5.3 and 5.5 will also need to be made.

Project personnel often have to learn a project management system the hard way, in the middle of a negotiation. Waiting until the last minute to learn a system can be a costly mistake. In order to

Table 5.7. Learning curve worksheet.

1. Please select the item below that best describes the computer experience of the scheduling software user(s) at your office.
   a. Never touched a computer before. (80 hours)
   b. Use of computers for word processing. (40 hours)
   c. Frequent use of database and spreadsheets. (24 hours)
   d. Developed application programs. (16 hours)
   e. Previous use of scheduling software. (8 hours)
2. Please select the number of activities in the largest project (as you did previously in Table 5.3) from the list below.
   a. Under 200 activities. (16 hours)
   b. Between 200 and 1000 activities. (24 hours)
   c. Over 1000 activities. (32 hours)
3. Please select the office type (as you did previously in Table 5.5) from the list below.
   a. Owner or owner's representative. (8 hours)
   b. Construction manager. (16 hours)
   c. Construction contractor. (32 hours)
4. Time required to learn the scheduling software that is most appropriate for your office is based on the addition of points from items one, two, and three of this table. Fill in the blanks below and calculate the amount of time that you will need.
   a. Hours from item one = _____
   b. Hours from item two = _____
   c. Hours from item three = _____
   d. Total hours (a+b+c) = _____
      is an estimate of the total number of hours required to learn the system.

determine the amount of time required for the office to learn to use the scheduling software needed for the office, proceed to Table 5.8. Table 5.8 indicates the amount of time that the scheduler should plan to learn the system. Each item in the table has a number of hours associated with it. The total hours from each item equal the estimated time necessary to learn the system.

If the time allowed to learn the system (from Table 5.8, item four) does not equal, or exceed, the time required to learn the system from Table 5.7, item four, then the scheduling system will not be mastered, and it can not be used efficiently.

Table 5.8. Time allowed to learn the software.

1. When does the scheduler need to start working with the schedule on a day-to-day basis?
   - a. In the next several months.   (160 hours)
   - b. Within the month.   (40 hours)
   - c. Immediately.   (0 hours)
2. Which one of the following statements best describes your offices manual use of CPM?
   - a. Never used any form of CPM.   (60 hours)
   - b. Took a CPM course.   (20 hours)
   - c. Used a manual CPM schedule to manage construction.   (0 hours)
3. Which one of the following statements best describes your scheduler's manual use of CPM?
   - a. Never used any form of CPM.   (60 hours)
   - b. Took a CPM course.   (20 hours)
   - c. Used a manual CPM schedule to manage construction.   (0 hours)
4. The estimated time allowed for learning the scheduling system is obtained by adding the hours from items one, two, and three:
   - a. Hours from item one =   _____
   - b. Hours from item two =   _____
   - c. Hours from item three =   _____
   - d. Total hours (a+b+c) =   _____

Personnel Turnover

The ability of the construction office to utilize sophisticated project management system features will be severely limited if there is high personnel turnover. There are several ways, however, to minimize the problems caused by high turnover. One way is to implement a project management system that is very easy to use. If the office's project load dictates that a more sophisticated system must be chosen, then purchasing a system that allows customization of menus, reports, and macros, is a good alternative. This second alternative, while requiring development time for system customization, will (in the long term) be the most effective for the office with high staff turnover. Table 5.9 assists the user in evaluating the software features required to support an office with a high turnover rate.

Table 5.9. Staff turnover worksheet.

1. If the staff using the scheduling software frequently change during the course of the project, then the following features should be considered:
   a. Scheduling software should provide the user to specify a set of reports, or commands to generate those reports, that may be used throughout the project.
   b. Scheduling software may provide features to customize reports to meet specific office requirements.
   c. Scheduling software may provide features to customize the systems user interface to meet the office's specific requirements.

Separate Project Sites

Because reporting consistency is very important at multiple project sites, the office that has separate sites needs to consider project scheduling systems that allow significant customization. This customization will provide efficient and consistent use of the system by the office staff. Consistent use of the project management system in separate sites is very important, because it allows personnel at various levels of command to communicate. As an alternative to customizing systems for each site, minicomputer and mainframe systems may be used to provide a central point for information storage and exchange. Table 5.10 evaluates the location of personnel who will need scheduling data.

Available Computer Systems

The cost of the microcomputer technology necessary to use a project management system is generally insignificant, when compared to the cost of change orders issued on large projects. While the purchase of hardware may seem significant, users will gain greater efficiencies if the proper equipment is available. There are three computer-related issues that the construction office should be aware of prior to reviewing any software. These are the operating system, random access memory, and hard disk storage.

   With the widespread use of personal computers, many software vendors have targeted their sales to the operating system. Several

Table 5.10. Evaluating user locations.

1. Which statement best describes the way that scheduling will be used at your office?
   a. All scheduling will be accomplished from a central location independent of actual project locations.
   b. Scheduling is to be accomplished at a number of independent project offices that report to a central office.
   c. All Scheduling will be accomplished from an office that directly works on these projects.
2. If scheduling from a central office, independent of project locations, you may wish to consider the following items:
   a. The purchase of microcomputer hardware and software, compatible with the home office equipment, which allows local use of schedule data.
   b. If the purchase of additional hardware and software is not feasible, then:
      (1) Provide standard reports and printed bar charts, which should be provided every two weeks.
      (2) Project personnel should be able to request ad hoc reports with a turnaround of less than two days.
      (3) Standard procedures should be developed to insure the timeliness and accuracy of scheduling data.
      (4) Biweekly progress meetings should be held, with the scheduler present, to review ongoing work.
3. If scheduling from one office, which takes care of several of projects, you may wish to consider the following items:
   a. The purchase of microcomputer hardware and software, compatible with the home office equipment, which allows local use of schedule data.
   b. If the purchase of additional hardware and software is not feasible, then:
      (1) All of item 2.b. above.
      (2) The purchase of hardware that allows remote dial-in and operation of scheduling software.
4. If scheduling from an office that is directly managing the construction, no additional features should be required.

software manufacturers have developed systems for a variety of operating systems, although the Disk Operating System (DOS) is the most common. Even if members of the construction team use different operating systems, many vendors provide products that translate between operating systems.

Random Access Memory (RAM), typically expressed in thousands of bytes or kilobytes (KB, or simply K), represents the amount of processing space available to execute programs. The standard

IBM or compatible computer with an INTEL 80286 processing chip has 512 KB of memory. Under DOS, many project scheduling systems take up a larger amount of memory space (640 KB). Increasing the memory from the standard 512 KB to 640 KB is generally inexpensive. The use of memory-resident programs, or Local Area Networks, may prohibit many larger project management system from running.

The concurrent use of memory-resident programs with scheduling programs will require the purchase of additional extended or expanded memory and a memory manager. Many primarily microcomputer-based scheduling systems do not support extended or expanded memory at this time.

Storage of the project management system and project files may be done either on floppy disks or within the computer itself, on a hard disk. Many project scheduling systems require that the computer have a hard disk. The hard drive is an extremely useful device and might have to be purchased eventually, in any event. Sufficient disk space must be available on existing hard disks. Project scheduling systems typically require between 1 MB (megabyte, or million bytes) and 5 MB, excluding project files.

Efficient scheduling also requires that the user have access to the computer. Computers that are used by clerical workers for word processing are completely inadequate, since scheduling engineers will not be able to use the project management system. Table 5.11 identifies the computer hardware requirements for the example project.

Frequently, there are not enough computers in a construction office to use a scheduling system efficiently. While the ideal case is that each person who needs to use a scheduling system have access to their own desktop computer, this is often not the reality in a construction office. Having to share time on the computer among several personnel at the office will doom scheduling program use to crisis situation use only. The lack of "available on demand" computing power is one of the most important and most easily remedied problems in the implementation of project scheduling systems. Many owners have recognized the importance of proper planning and, considering the comparatively insignificant cost of today's microcomputers, are generally willing to provide funds to purchase or lease hardware and software for scheduling.

Table 5.11. Hardware availability worksheet.

1. If your office does not own, or is not leasing, a microcomputer, then the *minimum* requirements for such a system must include the following:
   a. Intel 80286 processor (fully IBM PC/AT compatible).
   b. Disk Operating System (DOS).
   c. Ten megabyte (10 MB) hard disk storage space.
   d. One 360 kilobyte (360 KB) floppy disk drive.
   e. 640 kilobytes (640 KB) of Random Access Memory (RAM).
   f. Color monitor (preferably EGA or VGA) and graphics card.
   g. Parallel port (for printer).
   h. Wide carriage printer with double strike and compressed capability.
   i. Plotter, if plotted charts are required.
2. If the scheduling software will be installed on a computer that is shared by several people, then you should purchase another computer for scheduling.
3. Verify that your computer's operating system matches the operating system of the scheduling system selected.
4. If your system uses the DOS operating system, and you have less than 640 Kilobytes (640 KB), of Random Access Memory (RAM), then you should purchase enough memory to support your scheduling system.
5. Determine the amount of hard disk space required by the scheduling system and the amount of memory required per activity. From these numbers and the data contained in Table 5.1, determine the minimum amount of free disk space required.
6. If you are scheduling projects over 1000 activities, then you should purchase a math coprocessor (if supported by the selected software).
7. If you need to use plotted charts, then you will need to consider the following items:
   a. That all cables required to operate the plotter are obtained.
   b. All technical reference material on the plotter must be obtained.
   c. The scheduling software must have a user support hot-line to assist in setting up or using your plotter. This service should have a model of your plotter to test if you encounter problems.
8. If your system does not have an EGA or VGA monitor and graphics card, then the purchase of this enhanced graphics capability will increase your office's scheduling efficiency.

Selection Summary

Identifying scheduling software/hardware features that support the office's scheduling efforts, using Tables 5.1 through 5.11, will save significant time in choosing the right software. Using the selection method will also assist in identifying the impacts that scheduling may have on the office, as well as providing the scheduler with the ability to justify the need for each specific software feature or for additional hardware. Reading Chapters Two through Five will also assist in explaining the usefulness of these features in a practical office setting.

THE EXCHANGE OF SCHEDULING DATA

One of the most often heard reasons for not using scheduling at the owner or owner's representatives' offices is that the time required to reenter the data, possibly into several different scheduling systems, is not worth the effort. Fortunately, many scheduling systems allow data to be imputed from a data file. This data file may be exchanged between members of the construction team on floppy disks or over networks or telephone lines. Including the exchange of scheduling data in construction specifications will greatly reduce the time required for manual data analysis and increase the ability of all team members to work with the same scheduling data.

Using the Same Scheduling System

The easiest method of data exchange is for all members of the project team to use the same scheduling software. While this is not possible for many projects, for very large projects it may be cost-effective for all project offices to purchase the same hardware and software specifically for that project. This arrangement can often be made informally between members of the construction team. Some guidelines, however, need to be followed if the data exchange is to be successful.

The basic premise of any scheduling system data exchange is that the data on the disks must exactly match the data that is provided in written reports. Due to the time that may be required to produce several sets of reports, or for any number of other possible reasons, the data on the reports may be slightly modified from the data on which the report was developed. When the data on the reports differs from that submitted on the data disk, confidence in the data exchange falls. Insuring data integrity must not be left up to an informal agreement.

The most effective way to insure data integrity is to make one party of the team responsible for production, distribution, and maintenance of all data and reports. First, designating one responsible party will insure that there is only one "official" schedule, regardless of the number of electronic versions produced in the past, for whatever reason. Secondly, if there is any variation between the printed and electronic data, then the problem can be resolved by the designated responsible party.

Maintaining several "copies of record" for each official schedule distributed is of critical importance to effective data exchange. Often, several months into a large project, some earlier schedules will need to be moved to floppy disks, in order to save hard disk space. Since most electronic data is sensitive to environmental factors, the party responsible for maintaining the schedule of record must keep multiple sets of backup disks at different locations. Even several backups in one location is sufficient to insure that the scheduler would not have to retype several thousand activities for several different schedules if data is lost. A prudent scheduler might, therefore, send backup copies of the official schedule to a headquarters office, their home, and to another member of the construction team.

Another important aspect of maintaining copies of the electronic schedule data is the ability to keep track of when various schedule versions were created. If a fixed number of characters for schedule identification numbers is provided by the software, then the worst alternative to naming schedule versions is to use one schedule name and update that same schedule throughout the project. If this approach is taken, then every scheduler will be required to spend up to two person-days per month to rename and back up schedule versions. In addition, the scheduler may never be quite sure which schedule version is loaded at any given time.

Since some scheduling systems only allow for a four character code to designate the schedule creating date, looking at a long list of these four character schedule designations may not immediately provide a clear indication of what schedule reflects which update. Some type of naming convention should be designated. Even some of the most clear conventions may, however, be unsatisfactory. For example, if it was agreed to name the schedule by the day and month of the data date, as in "1302" for the thirteenth of February, or by the month of the data date, as in "FEB," and the project extended over more than one year, then there could be conflicts. Using the number of the update may be the only satisfactory alternative. With this convention, schedule "0000" would be the initial schedule, "0001" would be the first update, etc. Even with this scheme, there are problems. For example, what should you do if some schedule submissions need to be revised; would revised versions receive new submission numbers or maintain the same numbers and overwrite previous schedule submission?

Regardless of the schedule identification number naming conventions agreed upon by the members of the project team, the scheduler will need to utilize a legend that identifies the exact schedule version, the data date, and the file creation date. While the party responsible for maintaining the schedule of record will keep the official version of this schedule in a version log, each scheduler may need to review previous schedules and should maintain their own logs. Each scheduler may also create several different "what-if" type schedules, for the analysis of specific project issues. Each of the schedules should also be logged and saved.

Another area that may cause problems in the direct exchange of scheduling system data are various types of calculation methods for dates and costs. Table 5.12 provides a list of these types of methods, which should be agreed upon prior to any electronic data transfer.

Either in scheduling specifications or during preconstruction meetings, the items noted in the table above must be resolved prior to the first submission of a network. Another set of factors to be resolved at the very beginning of the project is the level of detail of schedule activities. Table 5.13 lists several additional issues that should be addressed in contract specifications or in the initial meetings.

The items to be reviewed noted to this point pertain to topics that

Table 5.12. Calculation method checklist.

1. Will activity durations be based on a five- or seven-day workweek?
2. Will multiple calendars be used?
3. What holidays will be used for which calendar(s)?
4. Will activity progress be allowed without an Actual Start Date?
5. Will activity completion be allowed without an Actual Finish Date?
6. Will out-of-sequence progress be allowed?
7. If there are intermediate milestones that should be included in the schedule, then how will the introduction of "plugged" dates effect schedule calculation?

Table 5.13. Activity detail checklist.

---

1. Will the payment period be the basis for determining appropriate activity duration?
2. What activity codes and values will be used for schedule activities?
3. To what extent will procurement activities be included in the construction schedule?
4. To what extent will the inclusion of several different trades or types of materials be allowed in one activity?

---

govern technical aspects of the schedule, other items defining the way the schedule is used and how changes are to be posted to the network should also be agreed upon prior to starting the project. Table 5.14 includes a checklist of factors used to assist in the proper use of the schedule during the contract.

Even if all members of the project team utilize the same scheduling system, there are many practical considerations, both in the calculation of the schedule and the practical use of the schedule, that should be resolved prior to using any scheduling system. When members of the project team do not use the same scheduling system, which is often the case, then even more issues need to be addressed.

Table 5.14. Schedule use checklist.

---

1. Are the qualifications of scheduling personnel adequate for this particular project?
2. What specific electronic media will be used to provide the electronic schedule data?
3. When will the first detailed schedule need to be completed?
4. Will payment be based on the progress shown on the schedule?
5. Will time and cost completion be determined independently?
6. Will schedule changes need to be approved prior to schedule updating?
7. Will periodic progress meetings be held to review schedule changes?
8. What paper reports will be required for the periodic schedule update?
9. Under what circumstances will the schedule changes be paid for by the owner or owner's representative? By other members of the project team?
10. To what extent will the schedule be used as a means to justify requests for time extensions to the contract?
11. Under what circumstances can which project team members use an activities float without compensating the other parties?

Specifying a Data Exchange Standard

When specifying a data exchange format, the key issues to be resolved are the amount of scheduling data that is required to monitor and control the project, the exact data format of each data, and the exact definition of each element. The U.S. Army Corps of Engineers, Construction Engineering Research Lab (CERL), has been working with all sectors of the construction industry and many software manufacturers, with the intent of developing one standard data exchange format.

During the initial data exchange workshop held at CERL on August 1988, several assumptions and requirements were identified an essential for developing a useful construction industry standard. One assumption on which the standard should be based upon is that the scheduling information needs of small construction projects are not as comprehensive as those in larger projects. Another assumption is that optional records are provided for larger construction projections. The first requirement of the current standard is that it should be capable for use with as many scheduling systems, and as little reprogramming, as possible. The second requirement is that it should be flexible enough to apply to as many construction offices as possible. Finally, the standard should be based upon a complete transfer of all data elements at every update period. The version of the format and sample specifications that might be used to govern the use of the format is in Appendix A.

The goal of developing the project management system data exchange standard is to allow project scheduling systems to easily share information with other programs. Although the current focus of the data exchange standard is to transfer scheduling data between various scheduling software, other uses for the standard include integrating scheduling data into other automated systems used at the construction office.

INTEGRATION OF SCHEDULING AND OTHER SYSTEMS

As the format for scheduling data becomes more standardized, the integration of schedule data into other computerized construction systems will occur more frequently. Two types of applications that may be easily integrated with the scheduling data exchange standard are procurement and submittal register systems. These systems, typically used to track material submittal, approval, manufacture, and delivery, are frequently used in construction offices. Since delays in the procurement process frequently delay construction, integrating the procurement and submittal due dates into the construction CPM will allow these activities to be monitored with the construction activities they effect. Since a late delivery or submittal would delay the start of related construction activities, the project manager should have this information within his CPM.

A system that uses data from procurement, submittal, and scheduling systems will be able to identify potential delays due to the late arrival of materials. Only four data elements, of the potentially numerous data elements in a procurement or submittal system, need to be extracted to perform the schedule comparison. The first three elements are the submittal number, the description of the submittal, and the expected material delivery date. The last submittal data element required to fully integrate submittal into a CPM is the activity number of the potentially impacted construction activity that requires the submittal material.

Once the impacted construction activity has been identified, a program may be written in any number of widely available data base application programs that compares the material delivery dates against the activity's early start date. The report generated from this comparison will identify those material delivery dates from the procurement system that may delay construction activities.

Preparing a small program for this comparison should take only a few days for anyone with even limited experience in data base application programming. The next step in the development process would be to develop a more sophisticated report that would identify those activities that may actually produce a schedule change input file. The input file could create a "what-if" version of the current construction schedule and automatically update the delayed activities, with their new start dates based on the procurement and submittal systems. Once these dates are updated, the schedule may be recalculated using the scheduling software, and the impact of all late submittal for the entire project could be rapidly identified.

Data from other types of existing data systems, such as payroll and accounting systems, may also be tied to scheduling data. Payroll systems typically contain the resources used during some specified period. This data may be used to automatically update the resources used for each schedule activity. Cost sheets for each employee would be coded according to the type of work (and activity) that occurred during that period. Schedule activities cost control fields can then be summed for payments and provide information to accounting systems for the generation of invoices.

Many scheduling systems allow direct access of, or output of, schedule data to the most commonly used data base and spreadsheet programs. Systems that have this capability may provide rapid integration of scheduling data with related office project control systems, if the related systems were developed with commonly used data base and spreadsheet programs.

EVALUATING CHANGES AND CLAIMS WITH CPM

Members of the construction team are expected not to delay or hinder each other's efforts to complete a project in a timely fashion.[3] There are, however, many situations that arise during construction projects between owners and contractors that do impact on the timely completion of construction. These situations are usually the result of the owner's direct request for additional work, called changes, or the result of an owner's actions, which in some way increase the contractor's costs, called claims. Several specific examples of potential claim situations are: (1) giving directions to start a portion of work where there are known delays, (2) stopping payments that are keeping the job going, (3) directing work to proceed in a piecemeal basis or at times other than was originally planned, (4) other parties interfering with the work, (5) failing to coordinate the work of outside contractors at the prime contractor's convenience, (6) failure to provide timely information, (7) failure to disclose pertinent knowledge, and (8) failure to provide owner-furnished equipment on a timely basis.

One mark of a good project team is the ability to resolve changes and claims without resorting to legal proceedings. Knowing the legal

---

[3]Wickwire, Jon M., Hurlbut, Stephen B., and Shapiro, Lori R., "Rights and Obligations in Scheduling: Basic Principals and Guidelines," Construction Briefings, No. 88-13, Federal Publications, December 1988. pg. 2.

rights and responsibilities of each party before the situation results in a legal proceeding will most likely reduce the number of times that the parties are forced to go to court. While not meant to be a legal treatise, this section discusses the practical steps that can be taken, based on legal precedents, that may be used to justify or affirmatively defend claims and changes disputes.

Since a well-constructed CPM is a "snapshot" of planned and as-built progress throughout a project, the CPM has been effectively used to evaluate the impact of changes and claims on construction projects. The CPM will accurately reflect project impacts only if it is utilized to develop a correct initial schedule and regularly updated.

Judges have provided some insight into the use of CPM in their decisions. The Board in *Continental Consolidated Corp.* succinctly stated its position in using CPM for changes and claims when it held:

It is essential that any changes in the work and time extensions due to the contractor be incorporated in to the progress analysis concurrently with the performance of the changes or immediately after the delay and this integrated into the periodic computer runs to reflect the effect on the critical path. Otherwise, the critical path chart produced by the computer will not reflect the current status of the work performed or the actual progress being attained.[4]

In *Preston-Brady Co. vs Veterans Administration*, the court stated another axiom for using CPM schedules:

A general statement that disruption or impact occurred, absent any showing through use of updated CPM schedules, Logs or credible and specific data or testimony will not suffice (to prove a contractor's claim).[5]

Based on these and other statements made by the courts, six ways to effectively use CPM can be identified.[6] These principles, while

---

[4]Engineering Board of Contract Appeals Cases (ENGBCA Nos.) 2743 and 2766, 67-1 BCA 6624.
[5]VABCA Nos. 1892, et al., 87-1 GAC Section 19,649 at 99,520.
[6]Wickwire, Jon M., Walstad, Paul J., and Asselin, Thomas H., "Project Scheduling: Principals, Applications, and Problems," Federal Publications, No. 75-5, October 1975. p. 7.

dependent upon the exact language of every construction contract, are generally applicable to most projects. The first of these six principles is that as-planned CPM presentations must reflect a reasonable sequence of work. Second, a CPM analysis must be based upon, and be consistent with, project records. Next, a CPM analysis must be based upon reasonable activity durations and appropriate relationships between activities. The fourth scheduling principle is that the CPM must not contain any mathematical errors. The fifth is that, if expert testimony is utilized, then the expert must have reviewed the data upon which the CPM analysis is based. Finally, the CPM analyses must properly identify, evaluate, and relate delays to the specific scheduling activities.

To apply these six scheduling axioms, there are three distinct schedules needed to justify compensation for changes and claims. The first is a correct initial schedule that illustrates the contractor's original plan to complete the project. If appropriate, the owner's approval of this initial schedule should also be cited.

The second schedule that needs to be developed is one that shows what would have happened to the project if the change or claim had not occurred. This schedule will be an updated version of the initial schedule up to the point at which the change or claim situation occurred. Although after-the-fact schedules can be used, if logically correct and conforming to the six principles outlined above, they are very expensive to properly reconstruct, since all past project records must be obtained and evaluated. The after-the-fact schedules are also more easily attacked, since they contain limited information.

The schedule reflecting the status of the project at the time of the change or claim should clearly show all previously agreed-upon changes, contractor delays, and any changes in durations and all logic changes. One type of important logic change frequently omitted in periodic schedule updates is that of removing constraints that will not actually restrain future construction progress. When developing the second schedule to reflect the status of the project at the time that the change or claim occurred, unnecessary schedule constraints should also be removed.

The final schedule needed to justify time for changes and claims is the schedule that includes the change or claimed work. The differences in this schedule, compared to the updated initial schedule, will highlight the impact of the changes or claims.

The analysis of the activities of direct changes, using the three types of schedules, is often straightforward. All activities to be added, deleted, or modified are identified. The changes to specific activities agreed upon by the construction team, and the schedule based on the changes, may then be produced. Changes to construction schedules will often require that the contract duration be extended.

Time extensions to the construction schedule will usually be required if activities on the critical path are changed due to new work. Changes in noncritical activities may also indicate a time extension, if the changes are of such a magnitude as to move the critical path to the previously noncritical activities. The impact of changes to project completion must also be evaluated in light of other delays to the project. The impact of contractor-caused delays in starting or completing activities must be evaluated simultaneously, to see what actually caused the change in contract completion. Unless the changed work is the direct cause of the delay to the contract completion, a time extension may not be granted.

Determining the impact of the change on other aspects of the construction, or the impacts on other types of problems that occurred during the project, may be more difficult. There are two types of impacts that changes and claims may have on other aspects of the project. The first impact occurs if additional resources need to be added to activities to complete the schedule. This type of claim is called an acceleration claim. The second type of impact is decreased productivity of ongoing work. This type of claim is called a loss of efficiency claim.

The goal of the acceleration claim is to show that a member of the construction team was not given sufficient time to complete work directed by another member.[7] To clearly illustrate this type of claim, you need to show that additional resources were required to complete the work within the stated time. To justify this increased resource requirement, the party should show a detailed original resource plan, using the CPM's resource analysis features. The exact

---

[7]Wickwire, Jon M., Hurlbut, Stephen B., and Lerman, Lance J., "Use of Critical Path Method Techniques in Contract Claims: Issues and Developments, 1974 to 1988," Public Contract Law Journal, Vol. 18, No. 2, American Bar Association, March 1989. p. 355.

nature of the changes to every effected activity's manpower loading and logic must be identified and documented. To justify compensation for acceleration, the party will, typically, show that additional work within the same duration either had logic changes that required parallel efforts, or required additional resources.

Loss of efficiency increases labor costs due to delays in the project or the addition of new work that disrupts existing workers. If the original plan is substantially altered, subcontractors often are disrupted and may file loss of efficiency claims. Some of the specific types of schedule changes that may decrease crew efficiency include changes to crew chases, completely stopping ongoing work, starting the work at a later time, overtime work, resource loading activities that have insufficient physical space to handle the new resources, and performing work out-of-sequence so that rework needs to be done. Of course, loss of efficiency claims must also be directly attributable to the party in question, or the claim may not be awarded.

Using CPM to justify compensation for changes or claims should be a very detailed process, where the projected, or actual, impacts of new work are evaluated against the updated, correct original progress schedule. CPM data should be correlated to as many records as possible, including daily project logs, testing reports, submittals, invoices, and labor reports. The benefit of this detailed preparation of changes and claims is a rapid settlement of the matter, so that all parties will not have to go to court.

Chapter 6

Applying Advanced
Scheduling Techniques

INTRODUCTION

If you work with large schedules or are a full-time scheduling engineer, this chapter will provide you with some useful tools to assist in the creation and use of construction schedules. The first section discusses several important issues to be checked in generating or analyzing the initial schedule. The second section describes important analyses that should be considered during periodic schedule updates. Finally, a brief description on how resource allocation can be effectively applied to construction planning is provided.

SCHEDULE GENERATION

Practically speaking, the process of developing large construction schedules rarely follows the textbook approach of using a quantity take-off as the basis for schedule logic and activity durations. The traditional textbook approach assumes, unfortunately, that the project to be scheduled exists in a vacuum. Planning real construction projects requires a review of many aspects of the construction company's business, in addition to the current project to be scheduled. These aspects typically relate to the availability of critical resources. Several examples of critical resources are: the prime contractor's management team, subcontractors, and large contractor-owned equipment. The practical method of generating a construction plan, therefore, considers many issues outside of the project.

The availability of critical resources typically results in a schedule containing windows showing when the resources may work on the project being planned. When these windows are set, then the scheduler will develop a work plan to fit around the available resource windows. As a final check, the scheduler should review the resource windows to verify that sufficient resources have been allocated for all of the activities. Verifying that sufficient resources have been allocated is not often accomplished, due to time constraints placed on the scheduler. If sufficient resources are not allocated, the project will fall behind schedule.

Experienced schedulers use *rules of thumb* for generating initial schedules and for rapid schedule analysis. The rules of thumb for initial schedule generation and analysis fall into seven categories. These categories are: the general conditions, defining appropriate activities, activity durations, schedule logic, the critical path, the float, and cost. While not all of these "rules of thumb" are applicable for every project, they are generally applicable for 95 percent of all construction projects. The following subsections describe some of the rules of thumb. A more complete listing of these rules may be found in Appendix B.

General Conditions

One of the most important considerations when developing a network is that the network should reflect the general conditions of the construction contract. Included in the general conditions are those items that should be considered when starting to plan any construction project.

The most obvious general project conditions are the project start and finish dates. The schedule must begin on the *Notice to Proceed* (NTP) date and complete on or before the completion date. There are, however, several items that the scheduler should consider regarding the NTP and completion dates. The first item to consider is the way in which each of these dates should be "plugged" into the network. Care must be taken when these plugged-in dates are used, since they may alter the schedule's critical path without a clear warning to the scheduler. Secondly, intermediate project completion dates should be "plugged" into the network, as required. The effects of these intermediate dates on the schedule should also be checked.

Other general considerations refer to ways to set up a network that will make later analysis, using scheduling software, easier. First, activity identification numbers should use consecutive integers separated by a minimum of five numbers. Using letters in an activity identification number will, typically, be very confusing, especially if you do not spend full-time working on the schedule. Consecutive numbers should be used because they provide an easy way to trace through activities. Although many scheduling systems will now allow the use of characters and nonsequential activity identification numbers, using these features will usually require that the scheduler to spend more time analyzing and maintaining the network than on a sequential integer activity numbering scheme.[1]

Separating the activity identification numbers by a minimum of five numbers will allow for activities to be added as the project progresses. Another activity numbering scheme is called *activity banding*. Banding allows you to rapidly distinguish between activities in different work areas. In the Spiral Court Apartment project, introduced in Chapter 4, the schedule was banded according to work areas. Activities on each floor could be identified by their identification numbers, for example, numbers on the first floor were between 100 and 199, those on the second floor were between 200 and 299, etc.

The final general conditions that should be considered prior to entering any activity data are the activity descriptions and activity coding. The rule of thumb for activity descriptions is that descriptions should utilize a standard set of abbreviations or words. This standard set will allow you to communicate easily about the work involved in the activity. Using many different descriptions for the same type of work will confuse everyone, including a full-time scheduler. To avoid this problem, standardized coding schemes, such as the Construction Specification Index (CSI), or Building Systems Index (BSI), should be used to develop consistent activity descriptions.

Appropriate Activity Definition

This subsection deals with defining appropriate activities. These rules of thumb reflect contractual requirements and the level of

---

[1]While some experienced schedulers may prefer to use nonsequential and alphanumeric activity numbering, the casual user will be confused by this practice.

detail of activities. Determining the appropriate level of activity detail for a schedule is, generally, the most difficult aspect in generating networks. Guidelines in this subsection will assist you in developing a level of activity detail that will provide for both a control-level schedule and a management-level schedule.

Often, construction contracts and local building codes require contractors to conduct work according to some specific sequence. These sequences should be reflected in the schedule. For example, activities should be included for the acquisition of required permits. Specific activities should be included in the schedule for all contractually required milestones. Including these milestones is essential for adequate project control.

One of the most important rules for setting up a schedule is that of defining activities that may be easily related to one specific element of the construction project. Unless activities specifically reflect project components, the user will have a very difficult time using the schedule to control the project. Therefore, whenever an activity contains more than one type of work, trade, or material, the activity should be broken into its component parts. One breakdown often used is the submit, approve, procure, deliver, construct, and test sequence. This breakdown, as reflected in the Activity Type Code, will substantially improve your ability to anticipate non-construction-related problems. A correctly designed schedule should reflect differences in trade productivity. For example, three typical activities for interior partition construction are: metal studs, drywall, and drywall taping and finishing. All proceed at different crew productivity rates. Separating an "Install Partition" into "Install Metal Studs," "Install Drywall," and "Tape and Finish Drywall" will allow for a more concise estimate of the completion of the work, as well as more definitive control over potential problems. Typical areas where activity definition problems occur are in mechanical and electrical activities. These activities usually contain several different types of work lumped together. Since mechanical and electrical activities generally account for a majority of the problems on construction sites, these activities should be very carefully defined. More detailed breakdown activities should be developed from large activities that have components with different productivity rates.

An activity breakdown will often reflect differences in weather sensitivity, for example, drywall and taping. Drywall activities are sensitive to rain, while taping and finishing are more sensitive to humidity. Another example of weather-sensitive tasks that are often lumped together in a network are reinforcing steel and concrete placement. The reinforcing steel may be placed in cold weather, while the concrete placement may not proceed until ambient temperatures reach well above freezing.

Projects with repetitive types of work often have schedules that break tasks into several small activities, based on some arbitrary portion of the entire work. A large paving contract, therefore, might be split into "Top Course 33% Complete," "Top Course 67% Complete," and "Top Course 100% Complete." This type of breakdown does not, however, lend itself to easy reference on the project site. A more easily understood breakdown would be "Top Course Ash Ln to Fig Blvd," "Top Course Fig Blvd to Poplar St," and "Poplar St to Willow Ave." Using activity descriptions and breakdowns that allow direct relation of the schedule to physical construction elements will substantially enhance your ability to control the project effectively.

Once the level of detail necessary for project control has been included in the schedule, hammock activities may be used to summarize related categories of work. Summarizing these categories, based on a consistent and detailed control-level schedule, will provide the necessary management-level schedule. Attempting to derive project control information from a strictly management-level schedule will however, be completely inadequate.

Activity Durations

Since a contractor will want to get paid periodically, the schedule should reflect an activity breakdown that allows for rapid assessment of activity progress within the payment period. For example, if the contractor is going to request payment every 30 days, then the progress of a 120-day duration activity will be very difficult to assess. Since contractors are usually paid every 30 days, construction activities should, generally, range between 5 and 25 days.

Subcontract activities must also be fully integrated into a prime contractor's schedule. If subcontract activities have durations longer than 20 days, the subcontractor must be required to provide a fully integrated subnetwork. This subnetwork will break up large activities into smaller duration activities.

Finally, activity durations for all members of the construction team should be estimated. While a contractor will have the lion's share of the activities, other team members, such as the owner, architect, or city government, will also have tasks to accomplish. For example, owner's approval activities of contractor-certified items will, generally, be two weeks in duration. Architect/Engineer's approval activities will, generally, be between two weeks and one month in duration.

Due to the number of procurement actions that occur on a single project, it is impractical to include all procurement activities in the construction schedule. There are, however, many procurement activities that should be directly integrated with construction activities. One rule of thumb that is recommended is that all procurement actions over 60 days in length should be included as individual network activities, with submittal, approval, and delivery activities as well. Equipment or material that takes over 60 days to procure should be included in the schedule, due to the difficulty in obtaining alternative sources for the equipment or material if there is a procurement delay. The contractor will often, with materials that have a shorter procurement cycle, be able to find another supplier if there are delays.

Schedule Logic

Most guidelines creating accurate logic suggest the use of sets of repeating patterns of activities to develop schedule building blocks. Many of these blocks, often developed based on work areas, are connected to form a complete schedule. For example, the general progression of activities with long procurement durations should be submit, approve, procure, deliver, install, and test. An example of a pattern of activities that relates to building materials is steel structural framing. The construction of steel structures will generally be represented by the following series of activities: submit steel, approve steel, procure steel, deliver steel, erect steel, install metal deck, install deck slab, and fireproof steel. Other examples of material-based processes are cast-in-place concrete, precast concrete, and interior building partitions. The construction of cast-in-place structures will generally be represented by the following series of activities: submit concrete certification, submit rebar certification, submit concrete placement plan, approve concrete submittal, procure concrete materials, rebar delivery, install concrete forms, install rebar, install concrete, cure concrete, strip concrete forms, and move concrete forms. The construction of precast structures will generally be represented by the following series of activities: submit precast drawings, approve precast drawings, fabrication precast, deliver precast, install precast panels, install precast tie strips, install caulking, and seal precast. The installation of interior partitions may be represented by the following series of activities: submit drywall partition system, approve drywall system, procure drywall system, deliver drywall system, install metal studs, install drywall, install drywall taping.

The generation of schedules for projects that have repetitive or similar components is greatly simplified if you use sets of typical activities and merely change the activity identification numbers based on the work area of the activity. Several scheduling systems even allow you to duplicate, renumber, and add a set of repetitive activities back into the network. The Spiral Court Apartment project (Chapter 4) was created with a set of eighteen first floor activities that were copied and renumbered for each new floor.

Since mechanical work often delays construction projects, many schedulers have guidelines for scheduling mechanical activities. For example, mechanical rooms should be scheduled as early as possible to give access to the installation crews. Mechanical testing activities should also be checked to insure that all necessary utilities and a building load will be available to conduct the required testing.

Exterior closure is one of the most important construction milestone on most projects. The last three scheduling "rules of thumb" relating to schedule logic can assist in determining whether the building closure is adequately represented in the schedule. In high- and midrise buildings, the building skin of the first and second floors should generally be scheduled last. Exterior closure should incorporate separate activities for building "skin" and window installation. In some cases, sealing and caulking the exterior after window installation should be separately identified.

Critical Path Analysis

One of the first benefits to be realized from automated scheduling is that the critical path will be automatically calculated without requiring tedious arithmetic. Since the critical path is, fundamentally, the most important reason for using scheduling, there are several rules of thumb that pertain to the review of the critical path.

All activities that have a float of one working week or less should be considered critical activities. This is because near-critical activities can become critical activities in a matter of days.

If more than three parallel critical paths exist, it is likely that some durations have been overstated. Although the nature of some projects requires that crew chases directly follow one another in exact sequence, often forcing multiple parallel critical paths, this type of schedule should be carefully reviewed to check crew sizing and productivity. Once crew sizing and productivity have been established, the reasonableness of the activity duration may be reviewed.

Another way to check that the schedule has not been skewed to show too many critical activities, is to check the ratio of critical to total activities. A high ratio of critical to total activities suggests that the float has been manipulated, a low ratio of critical to total activities suggests that there is too little detail on critical path activities. At this point, there does not appear to be any established ranges for the number of critical activities. However, comparing this ratio to that of past projects of a similar nature may assist in determining a reasonable range.

Float Analysis

In the previous subsection, the manipulation of the float to force more activities on the critical path was mentioned. In this subsection, two rules of thumb regarding reduction of too much float in the network are given. First, all activities with over 100 days of float should be investigated. Second, installation activities with over 100 days of float are not properly integrated into the schedule.

Cost Analysis

The creation and analysis of construction schedules will, to some extent, be dependent upon the project's type of contract requirements. There are, however, many common issues in developing costs that advanced schedulers have adapted into rules of thumb. These rules of thumb fall into two categories, costs of activities and the cost of a group or the entire schedule.

The first rule of thumb regarding activity costs is that no cost should be allowed on submittal or approval activities. Activity costs should range between 0.1 and 2.5 percent of the total contract amount. Unit prices and quantities of early activities should be the same as the prices and quantities of the same type of activity that occurs later in the project.

The most clear criterion for the schedule costs is that the total cost of all activities may not exceed the contract amount. One of the cost control issues frequently noted in construction contracts is that of cost loading. Most owners would like to make sure that the contractor is paying for project financing. Two rules of thumb have been developed to provide an initial check to see whether the schedule is correctly loaded. First, at 33 percent complete in time, the contractor should have received 25 percent of the contract amount. Secondly, at 66 percent complete in time the contractor should have received 75 percent of the contract amount. This payment schedule roughly fits within the archetypical "S-curve" for earned value. The "S-curve" is shown in Figure 6.1.[2]

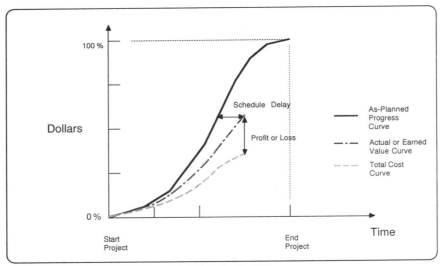

Figure 6.1. The classic "S" curve.

[2]Wiest, Jerome D. and Levy, Ferdinand. *A Management Guide to PERT-CPM With GERT-PDM, DCPM & Other Networks*, 2nd Ed. 1977. Englewood Cliffs, NJ: Prentice-Hall. This provides a good analysis of Figure 6.1.

ANALYSIS OF UPDATED SCHEDULES

Updating a construction schedule requires a meeting of the minds of the members of the construction team to assess the current project status. Updates should include the following: actual start dates for all activities showing any progress, remaining duration and earned value for all in-progress activities, and a final completion date for all activities with zero remaining duration. There are two key issues that must be addressed in the review of schedule updates. The first allows for a clear calculation of activity start and completion dates, the second, an unambiguous cost earnings statement.

Effective schedule updating requires a review of activity start dates, remaining durations, and completion dates, in every update period. From a computer calculation point of view, as described in Chapter Four, various scheduling software calculates activity completion dates differently, depending on the amount of information provided. The major complaint when making actual start and finish dates mandatory is that the actual start date of an activity is often not exactly known during the update meeting. While the exact date may not be known, an educated guess two weeks after the activities actual start may be far better than a wild guess during claim review time at the end of a project. To obtain the best estimate of start dates, the records of on-site project personnel should be reviewed.

The second issue in updating is how to provide or request a realistic payment invoice. When activities are substantially completed, but there remains some type of "punch list" work, warranty certifications, or submission of Operations and Maintenance manuals, special care is necessary. These substantially completed activities should be shown by having a remaining duration of zero days and an earned value less than the activity cost. This percentage of the activity cost can be withheld until the outstanding items are completed.

Similar to reviewing initial construction plans, experienced schedulers have developed a set of rules of thumb for the review of an in-progress schedule. The overall concept of an in-progress review is to determine whether the effective changes in the construction plan have already changed, or may in the future change, the final completion date, or violate of one of the initial scheduling constraints.

Frequently, when beginning schedulers review activities that have fallen behind schedule, they only review the particular activity that has fallen behind. Analysis of current progress should consist of monitoring the entire paths belonging to the lagging activity. This is very important, since the current delay may not only be the result of the currently delayed activities, but also the result of any one of the preceding path activities.

Experienced schedulers review the slippage between calculated schedule dates and actual dates on critical and near-critical activities, to identify schedule paths that could cause problems. Once a path has been identified as having missed the calculated schedule dates, then the experienced scheduler will attempt to determine the cause of the schedule slippage. Since schedule delays are known to have occurred, the initial analysis should be limited to those activities that have been completed or are currently in progress. Several different types of delays may be identified by the distinguishing characteristics shown in Table 6.1.

A common mistake made by beginning schedule reviewers is that they tend to look at delays as discrete items and do not consider productivity delays that may impact many similar activities later in the project. For example, if a rough-in plumbing activity was behind ten days, the typical response would be to reduce the duration of later activities by ten days. What the junior scheduler fails to recognize is that future plumbing activities may also be delayed due to poor crew productivity or an incorrect estimation of the initial duration.

Figure 6.2, below, shows an earnings curve for a project delayed by poor productivity. There are three cumulative cost curves in the

Table 6.1. Characteristics of delays.

1. Material procurement delays may be identified as a one-time occurrence, several delays with the same type of material, or a delay with all procurement leading up to a specific activity.
2. Weather delays may be identified by delays of similar activities along several paths through the schedule during discrete periods of time.
3. Subcontractor delays may be identified by identifying the performance factors by subcontract codes.
4. Productivity delays may be assessed by determining the projected man-hours per day to man-hours spent each day.

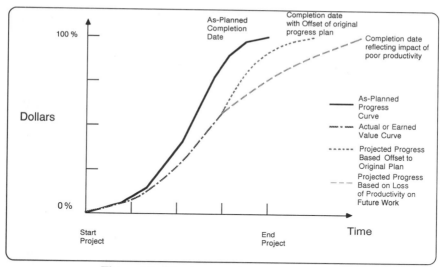

Figure 6.2. The impact of poor productivity.

figure. These three "S-curves" refer to the Original Plan, Actual Disbursements, and Projected Disbursements. From the figure, it can be seen that the actual progress, the darkened line, has fallen behind the originally planned progress, the solid line. The project is currently at month fifteen, and the scheduler is trying to predict when, based on the current status of the project, the project will be completed. The completion projected by scheduling software is simply a displacement of the original plan moved over to the current progress. The actual completion of the project, if the delays have been due to poor productivity, may be well behind the completion date projected by the scheduling software.

While the complete analysis of poor productivity is a very time-consuming process, given the current state of technology, this type of analysis should be conducted on suspected subsets of activities. The most rigorous way to identify poor productivity rates is to compare the actual duration of completed activities to the original duration. If one type of trade has, either on the average, or with some specific type of work, taken longer than expected, and this poor productivity trend is expected to continue, then this rate should be applied to all future work of a similar type, and a new schedule calculated. If these types of rates are not calculated for suspected problem trades or crews, then the scheduler may end up with a schedule that keeps slipping for no apparent reason until the contract completion date is well past due.

IDENTIFYING ACTIVITIES TO CRASH

When a schedule falls behind, there are several techniques that can be used to identify ways to make up the time. The simplest is to look for those activities on the critical path with long durations. These activities should be first candidates for making up lost time, since adding additional crews or equipment may reduce the duration of the activity and, therefore, reduce the length of the critical path.

Various options for increasing crew size may be used to perform rapid cost/time analysis. These analyses are conducted by modifying the duration of critical activities based on the various manpower loading options. The alternative that produces the lowest additional cost per saved day on the critical path can then be identified. Figure 6.3 shows how various options for manpower loading may effect the cost of the project. Figure 6.3 also indicates the number of days that could be saved on the project for each manpower loading option. If the additional cost and the number of days saved are graphed, as in Figure 6.3, then the least costly option for accomplishing the project can be identified.[3]

While the cost-time trade-off technique is very effective, there may be situations in which additional resources cannot be effectively utilized on critical activities. One example of an activity that may not be easily crashed is an activity in which electrical cable is pulled through a long underground conduit. Only a certain number of men and amount of cable-pulling equipment may be effectively used for this task. Adding additional workers to this activity may, in fact, extend the actual activity duration, since workers may end up interfering with each other.

In order to reduce the duration of critical activities that cannot efficiently use additional resources, the scheduler may attempt to reschedule sequential critical activities to run in parallel. For example, if the previous electrical cable-pulling has a manhole that provides additional worker access, the activity may be split into parallel

---

[3]Harris, Robert B. *Precedence and Arrow Networking Techniques for Construction*, 1978. New York: John Wiley & Sons. This provides a good analysis of the cost-time trade-off.

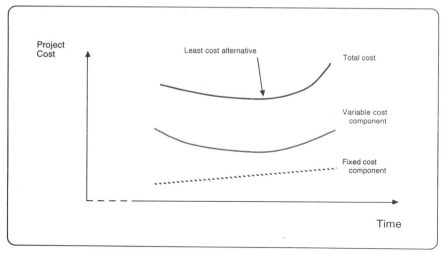

Figure 6.3. The cost-time curve.

fifteen-day cable-pulling activities, with an additional cable splicing activity of two days. Splitting a single long-duration activity, or running two separate activities, in parallel, rather than in a series, is a very effective technique for reducing the duration of a construction project.

Experienced project leaders typically apply these techniques to the activities of prime contractors prior to altering subcontractor activities. Coordinating the phasing of subcontractors on a construction project is very difficult, because the work has to be coordinated with both the project at hand and the subcontractors other on-going and planned projects. Altering the original subcontractor phasing plan may substantially disrupt the subcontractor's work, as well as the productivity of the contract work.

GENERATING SCHEDULES

The principles for reviewing schedules, outlined in the first and second sections of this chapter, may be effectively used to generate schedules for the control of construction projects. Scheduling software provides additional tools for assisting in the creation of complex construction plans. The following section will describe the most effective ways to make use of automated tools for schedule generation.

Automated Tools to Assist in Generating Schedules

The most important part of generating any construction plan is to visualize the project in terms of several similar work areas. As workers come on the project, they move in a steady progression from the first work area to the last work area. This type of smooth progression of trades, or "crew chases," is not found on all projects. However, the concept of separating work into definable parts should be used whenever possible. If activity data is entered into the network by work areas, the data can be available for rapid access. The work area code, described in the previous chapter, is one way in which the activity data may be coded to provide the ability to focus analysis efforts on specific portions of the project.

Scheduling software provides features for assisting the scheduler in arranging repetitive activities over several areas in the project. Many of the construction-oriented scheduling systems allow for the duplication of activities in a schedule. This duplication also allows for the scheduler to easily create activity numbers that correspond to various project work areas.

The Spiral Court Apartment project, described in detail in Chapter Four, was developed using the activity duplication process. First, the activities on the first floor were entered into the software. Next, the software was told to take the first floor activities, make a copy of these activities, and add 100 to their activity numbers. The process was repeated for each floor. The relative ease with which a person can fully and quickly grasp the Spiral Court Apartment project is caused by the duplication of the set of first floor activities. Using the duplication and renumbering feature, the scheduler need only remember a small set of activities (seventeen for Spiral Court) and the activity number coding scheme, rather than remember all of the activities in the network (one hundred and seventy four in the Spiral Court project).

Horizontal construction, such as highways, and other types of repetitive projects, are often scheduled in terms of the amount of material placed or percent completion. Each of these methods produces a schedule that makes it difficult to actually control the project and hides poor productivity. Using work areas to break

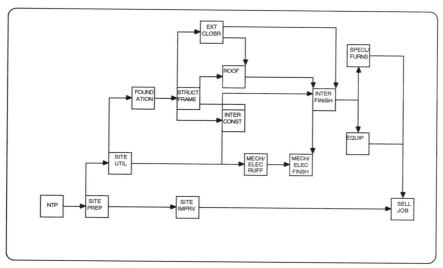

Figure 6.4. Skeletal project template.

down repetitive activities will greatly enhance scheduling efficiency for horizontal and other types of repetitive projects.

Additional Activity Definition Tips

The repetitive sets of activities that are copied and renumbered to form a complete schedule represents one type of "template" used in schedule generation. The experienced scheduler has templates of many types, which can be used on a wide number of projects. For example, from a macro-level, the construction of most buildings can be characterized by the template shown in Figure 6.4. This template contains the skeleton of all features contained in a building project.

When it comes to developing a detailed construction schedule, it seems that no two schedulers create the exact same network. The difference is generally due to differences in the way that people aggregate activities of the detailed trade and building material breakdowns into larger schedule activities. This aggregation is often greater in areas that the scheduler is unfamiliar with. For example, a civil engineer who may have specialized in geotechnical engineering will probably devote a great amount of detail to earth work and geotechnical investigation, and limit the amount of detail in mechanical and electrical work. Although procurement and mechani-

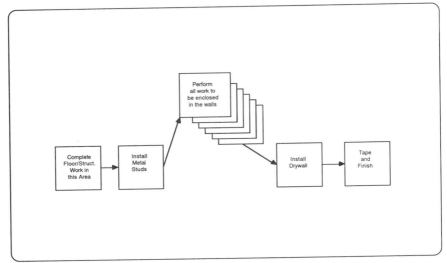

Figure 6.5. Template for partition installation.

cal and electrical problems are frequently the cause of delays, the geotechnical engineer will not, generally, add significant details to procurement, mechanical, and electrical work.

Experienced schedulers use a more detailed mental model of construction projects to fill out a schedule. These models, or templates, cover the general types of relations between building systems, trades, and construction materials. They often contain specific activities to deal with problems experienced on past projects. These specific activities are frequently related to the interrelationship of mechanical and/or electrical systems, the testing of building components, and the procurement of major equipment. Figure 6.5 is another example of a project template that, while not generally explicitly stated by experienced schedulers, is often used.

Generating useful construction schedules is both a science and an art. Creating a schedule with enough activities to accurately model the construction process, in order to monitor and control progress, while simultaneously maintaining a manageable level of schedule detail, often generates conflicting goals. If the scheduler begins to develop a schedule by generating consistent blocks of work and carrying those blocks through the project, with the appropriate activity codes, then there is a very good chance that the schedule can meet the conflicting goals of controlling construction progress and maintaining a manageable level of schedule detail.

SCHEDULES FOR MANAGEMENT

Schedules generally fall into two categories. The first category is the schedule for project control. This network contains sufficient detail for the proper monitoring and control of the construction process on a micro-level. The second category is the schedule for management reporting. The management-level schedule contains very few activities, which typically refer to less than twenty project milestones. Scheduling software available today has the capability to meet both of these needs in a single network.

The key to creating a successful construction control schedule is to develop a network that also monitors the activities that management is most interested in. In some projects, this is quite straightforward. For example, in the highrise construction project, the completion of each floor, exterior closure, and beneficial occupancy of the facility may be sufficient for management review. If the construction schedule is broken into activities by work area, the scheduler may create the management schedule by using "hammock" activities.

The duration of hammock activities is based on the time between the start of the first activity and the finish of the last activity attached to the hammock. If, in the Spiral Court Apartment project, for example, it is necessary to create a hammock activity to represent the completion of the first floor, then the activity would be tied to the start of activity 100, "Steel Framing and Pan Forms," and tied to the finish of activity 180, "Install Furnishings." Scheduling software insures that the duration of the hammock activity is based on the difference between these two dates. As the start of the first and the finish of the ending activity change, the dates and durations of the hammock activity also change. Table 6.2 shows a bar chart, with the first floor activities, single hammock activity, and the "Complete First Floor" shown at the bottom of the table. Table 6.3 shows a bar chart including only the hammock activities for each floor of the Spiral Court project. Table 6.4 shows a bar chart with hammock activities, showing the complete project broken down by major construction tasks.

Table 6.2. First floor bar chart.

ACTIVITY DESCRIPTION / ACT ID OD FLT	05 JAN 87	02 FEB 87	02 MAR 87	06 APR 87	04 MAY 87	01 JUN 87	06 JUL 87	03 AUG 87	07 SEP 87	05 OCT 87	02 NOV 87	07 DEC 87	04 JAN 88	01 FEB 88	07 MAR 88	04 APR 88
Steel Framing and Pan Forms / 100 5 0			EE / LL													
Steel Exterior Stairs / 103 1 25			E	L												
Place Concrete / 105 16 0			EEEE / LLLL													
Steel Studs / 110 8 10				EE	LL											
Wall Insulation / 115 5 57				EE			LL									
Electrical Rough-in / 120 7 55				EEE			LL									
Mechanical Rough-in / 125 14 10				EEEE	LLLL											

Interior Spiral
Steel Stairs
130   4   58   EE   LL

Install and Finish
Dry wall
135   7   45   EE   LL

Doors and
Hardware
140   8   61   EEE   LL

Paint
145   5   85   EE   LL

Exterior Siding
150   8   67   EEE   LL

Appliances and
Furnace
155   6   71   EE

Floor and Trim
160   3   86   EE   LL

Complete First
Floor
1100 61 91   L.

EEEEEEEEEEEE
LLLLLLLLLLLLLLLLLLLLLLLLLLLLLLLLLL

Table 6.3. Per floor bar chart.

ACTIVITY DESCRIPTION / ACT / OD / FLT	05 JAN 87	02 FEB 87	02 MAR 87	06 APR 87	04 MAY 87	01 JUN 87	06 JUL 87	03 AUG 87	07 SEP 87	05 OCT 87	02 NOV 87	07 DEC 87	04 JAN 88	01 FEB 88	07 MAR 88
Complete First Floor 1100 61 91	.	.	.	EEEEEEEEEEEE	LLLLLLLLLLLLLLLLLLLLLLLL			.			.		.	.	.
Complete Second Floor 1200 158 0	.	.	.	EEEEEEEEEEEEEEEEEEEEE	LLLLLLLLLLLLLLLLLLLLLL						.		.	.	.
Complete Third Floor 1300 153 0	.	.	.	.	EEEEEEEEEEEEEEEEEEEEEEE	LLLLLLLLLLLLLLLLLLLLLL					.		.	.	.
Complete Fourth Floor 1400 94 49	.	.	.	.	EEEEEEEEEEEE	LLLLLLLLLLLLLLLLLLLLLL					.		.	.	.
Complete Fifth Floor 1500 105 35	.	.	.	.	EEEEEEEEEEEEEEEE	LLLLLLLLLLLLLLLLLLL					.		.	.	.
Complete Sixth Floor 1600 116 21	.	.	.	.	.	EEEEEEEEEEEEEEEEEE	LLLLLLLLLLLLLLLLLL				.		.	.	.

Table 6.4. Overall project bar chart.

ACTIVITY DESCRIPTION	ACT	OD	FLT	07 JUL 86	04 AUG 86	01 SEP 86	06 OCT 86	03 NOV 86	01 DEC 86	05 JAN 87	02 FEB 87	02 MAR 87	06 APR 87	04 MAY 87	01 JUN 87	06 JUL 87	03 AUG 87	07 SEP 87	05 OCT 87	02 NOV 87
Notice To Proceed	2000	1	0	E L																
Submit and Procure Materials	2005	210	97			EEEEEEE	EEEEEEE	EEELLLLL	EEELLLLL	EEELLLLL	EEELLLLL	EEELLLLL	EEELLLLL	LLLLLLL	LLLLLLL	LLLLLLL				
Site Preparation	2010	16	127		EEEE						LLLL									
State Utilities	2015	22	299			EEEE							LLLLLLLLLLLLLLLLLLLLLLLL			LLL				
Foundation	2020	32	127			EEEEEE						LLLLLLL								
Site Improvements	2025	5	299				EE												L	
Structural Framing	2030	101	0											EEEEEEEEEEEEEE LLLLLLLLLLLLLLLL				L		
Interior Construction	2035	88	21												EEEEEEEEEEEEEEEEEE	LLLLLLLLL				
Mech and Elec Rough-In	2040	97	0												EEEEEEEEEEEEEEEEE					
Exterior Closure	2045	88	27												EEEEEEEEEEEEEE	LLLLLL		LLLLLL		
Roofing	2050	14	39															EEEE	LLL	
Mech and Elec Finish	2055	2	80												EE				L	

(continued)

Table 6.4. (continued)

ACTIVITY DESCRIPTION / ACT OD FLT	07 JUL 86	04 AUG 86	01 SEP 86	06 OCT 86	03 NOV 86	01 DEC 86	05 JAN 87	02 FEB 87	02 MAR 87	06 APR 87	04 MAY 87	01 JUN 87	06 JUL 87	03 AUG 87	07 SEP 87	05 OCT 87	02 NOV 87
Interior Finishes 2060 97 21	.	.	.	.	.	.	.	.	.	.	.	.	EEEEEEEEEEEEEEE		EEE	LLLLLLL	.
Specialties and Furnishings 2065 91 21	.	.	.	.	.	.	.	.	.	.	.	.	EEEEEEEEEEEEEE	EE	.	LLLLLL	.
Elevators and Temporary Hoist 2070 147 0	.	.	.	.	.	.	.	.	.	.	EEEEEEEEEEEEEEEEEEEEEEE		.	.	.	LL	.
Testing and Sell Job 2075 28 0	.	.	.	.	.	.	.	.	.	.	.	.	.	.	.	EEE	L

152

Using hammock activities may be confusing if they are not defined properly. Because hammock activities' durations may be very large, it is wise to uniquely identify hammock activities. One way frequently used is to select a band of activity numbers, at the very end of all schedule activities, to be used for this. In the Spiral Court project, the activity numbers between 1000 and 2075 were only used for hammock activities. Banding with hammock activities makes it easy to specifically identify activities for management reporting.

While hammocking activities is the preferred method for grouping activities for schedule analysis, grouping activities for cost and resource data may be accomplished by a feature called "activity summarization." Some software only provides summarization capability, without using hammock activities. Activity summarization allows the scheduler to obtain resource and cost summaries for resources, by grouping activities according to the value of specific activity code fields. Reports obtained with the activity summarization feature provide another perspective for schedule review.

ADDING RESOURCE DATA TO ACTIVITIES

Utilizing good techniques in generating and analyzing schedules will often allow the scheduler to anticipate many construction problems before they arise. The first resource problem that usually occurs when reviewing a schedule is that a single crew's work is not continuous through the project.[4] This problem, the crew chase design or unlimited resource allocation, will be covered in the first part of this section. The other problem that frequently occurs is that of limited resources. The limited resource allocation problem occurs either when there are insufficient resources to complete the work contained in a single activity within the allotted activity duration, or when there are several parallel activities that all require a limited resource. The limited resource problem will be discussed in the second part of this section. Several scheduling systems provide features for the definition of activities resource requirements, the calculation of cumulative resource requirements, and alternatives to assist in dealing with limited resources.

---

[4]For a rigorous discussion of the mathematics of resource analysis, see Harris, *Precedence and Arrow Networking Techniques for Construction* (1978).

Although many high-end scheduling programs provide some resource allocation and verification functions, these techniques are
often cumbersome to use. In addition, most scheduling systems
have their own terminology and somewhat different techniques for
resource analysis. Thus, the user must carefully check the resource
analysis provided by the system. Resource allocation techniques,
while extremely useful for a complete analysis of construction progress, will, for large construction projects, require a significant time
investment to master and utilize.

Resource coding may actually be thought of as a specialized type
of activity coding. Each activity may be assigned certain codes to
designate the types of crew and equipment that will be needed to
accomplish the task. Other code fields, also related to resources, may
also be provided by scheduling software. Some examples of these
fields are the number of crews planned to work on the activity, the
rate of production of a given crew, the quantity of material to be
produced during the duration of the activity, and equipment and/or
materials quantities necessary to produce the work.

The most versatile use of resource codes, as with activity codes,
allows the contractor to create a "library." This library may contain
production rates, materials, and equipment required for each crew,
which may be used on any project. Once crews are assigned to
specific activities, then the crew schedule, material lists, equipment
lists, and many cost-related reports can be generated.

Designing the Crew Chase

With all construction activities appropriately coded, the construction team can review the utilization of resources. On most projects,
the most efficient use of contractor personnel is to move crews to the
site and have them work at a steady rate until the work has been
completed. Once the work has been completed, the workers will
move on to another project. One of a contractor's worst nightmares
is having workers moved on and off of the project. This type of
staggered crew scheduling will significantly reduce worker productivity and should be avoided if possible.

To assist contractors in analyzing their crew allocation, many
project management systems include features that provide a listing
of daily worker requirements for any of the resource codes that are
part of the project. For example, a program may show the number

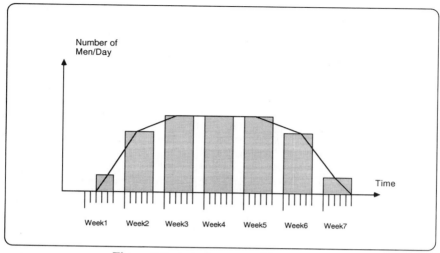

Figure 6.6. Actual resource histogram.

of carpenters required every day. The software presents this information through a bar chart, where each day or week is shown on the bottom of the graph, and the height of the bars represents the number of workers required per time period. This type of bar chart is called a histogram. Figure 6.6 shows a typical histogram pattern that is the most efficient. There are three levels of work force in the ideal histogram. The first group, in week one, mobilizes and starts a set of activities. The second group, from week two to week six, completes the bulk of the work on the project. The third crew, in week seven, completes punchlist items and cleans the work area. On most projects, only the second group of activities, completing the construction work, is actually modeled. Figure 6.7 shows an average resource histogram developed for most projects.

Resource allocations for an actual project will often not meet the ideal set of three levels for mobilization, completion of work, and punch list. This is because scheduling systems rely on the early or late start dates to calculate a schedule, and not on the optimum resource allocation. Tables 6.5 and 6.6 illustrate an inefficient resource allocation, from the Spiral Court project, for the concrete and metal studs crews.

Reviewing the bar chart in Table 6.6 shows the difference between a desirable and a poor crew chase. The concrete placement activities directly follow one another, and this allows the crew to move from

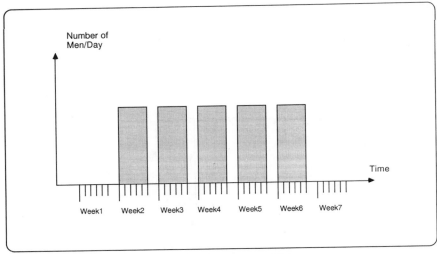

Figure 6.7. Averaged resource histogram.

one floor to the next without any delay. This type of crew chase is
very productive, requiring only one mobilization and demobiliza-
tion, and taking full advantage of the learning curve. The steel stud
activities, on the other hand, are an example of a crew chase predes-
tined to overrun budgeted costs. If all the steel stud activities begin
on their early start dates, then the crew will have to stop work and

Table 6.5. Concrete and metal stud activities.

ACT ID	ORG DUR	DESCRIPTION	EARLY START	EARLY FINISH	LATE START	LATE FINISH	FLOAT
105	16	Place Concrete	17MAR87	7APR87	17MAR87	7APR87	0
110	8	Steel Studs	8APR87	17APR87	22APR87	1MAY87	10
205	16	Place Concrete	8APR87	29APR87	8APR87	29APR87	0
210	8	Steel Studs	30APR87	11MAY87	12MAY87	21MAY87	8
305	16	Place Concrete	30APR87	21MAY87	30APR87	21MAY87	0
310	8	Steel Studs	22MAY87	3JUN87	2JUN87	11JUN87	6
405	16	Place Concrete	22MAY87	15JUN87	22MAY87	15JUN87	0
410	8	Steel Studs	16JUN87	25JUN87	22JUN87	1JUL87	4
505	16	Place Concrete	16JUN87	8JUL87	16JUN87	8JUL87	0
510	8	Steel Studs	9JUL87	20JUL87	13JUL87	22JUL87	2
605	16	Place Concrete	9JUL87	30JUL87	9JUL87	30JUL87	0
610	8	Steel Studs	31JUL87	11AUG87	31JUL87	11AUG87	0

Table 6.6. Split crew chase.

DESCRIPTION ID OD FLT	06 APR 87	13 APR 87	20 APR 87	27 APR 87	04 MAY 87	11 MAY 87	18 MAY 87	25 MAY 87	01 JUN 87	08 JUN 87	15 JUN 87	22 JUN 87	29 JUN 87	06 JUL 87	13 JUL 87	20 JUL 87	27 JUL 87	03 AUG 87	10 AUG 87
Place concrete 105 16 0	EEEEE																		
Place Concrete 205 16 0		EEEEEEEEEEEE																	
Place Concrete 305 16 0					EEEEEEEEEEEEEE														
Place Concrete 405 16 0								EEEEEEEEEEEEE											
Place Concrete 505 16 0												EEEEEEEEEEEEE							
Place Concrete 605 16 0															EEEEEEEEEEEEEE				
Steel Studs 110 8 10		EEEEEE																	
Steel Studs 210 8 8					EEEEEEE														
Steel Studs 310 8 6								EEEEEEEE											
Steel Studs 410 8 4												EEEEEEE							
Steel Studs 510 8 2															EEEEEEE				
Steel Studs 610 8 0																			EEEEEEE

Annotations on chart: DESIRABLE CREW CHASE; SPLIT CREW CHASE

157

Table 6.7. Nonsplit crew chase.

A Gantt chart (crew chase schedule) with the following activities and date columns:

DESCRIPTION	ID	OD	FLT	06 APR 87	13 APR 87	20 APR 87	27 APR 87	04 MAY 87	11 MAY 87	18 MAY 87	25 MAY 87	01 JUN 87	08 JUN 87	15 JUN 87	22 JUN 87	29 JUN 87	06 JUL 87	13 JUL 87	20 JUL 87	27 JUL 87	03 AUG 87	10 AUG 87
Place Concrete	105	16	0	EEEEE																		
Place Concrete	205	16	0		EEEEEEEEEEEEEE																	
Place Concrete	305	16	0					EEEEEEEEEEEEEE														
Place Concrete	405	16	0								EEEEEEEEEEEEEE											
Place Concrete	505	16	0												EEEEEEEEEEEEEE							
Place Concrete	605	16	0															EEEEEEEEEEEEEE				
Steel Studs	110	8	10										>EEEEEE									
Steel Studs	210	8	8												>EEEEEEE							
Steel Studs	310	8	6														>EEEEEEEE					
Steel Studs	410	8	4																>EEEEEEE			
Steel Studs	510	8	2																	>EEEEEEE		
Steel Studs	610	8	0																			EEEEEEE

Annotations: "DESIRABLE CREW CHASE", "REVISED CREW CHASE".

wait for the floor above to be completed. If the steel studs are being installed by subcontractors, then splitting activities is even worse, because the subcontractor may pull the workers off of the job.

A more productive and less costly solution to allocating resources for the steel stud construction is to allow the steel stud crew to come on-site later, after there is enough work completed for them to remain on-site from start to finish of their work. Table 6.7 graphically shows the revised schedule that provides a "nonsplit" solution for the resource allocation problem.

Using the "nonsplit" crew chase from Table 6.7 will dramatically increase productivity and reduce the cost of the steel stud installation. When developing the crew design for a complete project, each crew chase should be charted out and the optimum placement of activities for effective resource allocation determined.

Limited Resources

The previous discussion focused on the way to design a crew chase for optimum output. This crew design assumes, however, that there are sufficient workers to make up the crew, and that all materials are available when needed. This is often a very optimistic assumption. When resources are scarce, then limited resource analysis will help to determine the optimum placement of activities in a network to keep the project flowing, without requiring that too much work to be accomplished in too short a time.

In order to illustrate the limited resource problem, the example of several steel activities from the Spiral Court Apartment project that might require a crane will be used. Table 6.8 shows an example bar chart based on the early start of these activities. Table 6.8 may also be used to identify the requirement for crane use for these activities, since every day that more than one of these activities works, there will be a need for additional cranes. If all of the scheduled crews actually arrived on-site according to the schedule, then one of these crews would not work, or both of these crews would have substantial delays, due to the crane being split between two activities.

There are two alternatives for solving the limited resource problem: either get more resources or change the schedule to allow the work to proceed with as little disruption as possible with the existing limited resources. Scheduling software provides some assistance in

Table 6.8. Activities that might require a crane.

ACTIVITY DESCRIPTION				07 JUL 86	04 AUG 86	01 SEP 86	06 OCT 86	03 NOV 86	01 DEC 86	05 JAN 87	02 FEB 87	02 MAR 87	06 APR 87	04 MAY 87	01 JUN 87	06 JUL 87	03 AUG 87	07 SEP 87
ID	OD	FLT																
Steel Framing and Pan Forms												EE	LL					
100	5	0																
Steel Exterior Stairs													E	L				
103	1	25																
Place Concrete													EEEE					
105	16	0												LLLL					
Steel Studs													EE	LL				
110	8	10																
Interior Spiral Steel Stairs													EE	LL			LL	
130	4	58																
Steel Framing and Pan Forms													EE	LL	L			
200	5	11																
Steel Exterior Stairs														E	L			
203	1	34																
Place Concrete														EEEE				
205	16	0													LLLL				
Steel Studs															EEE	LL		
210	8	8																
Interior Spiral Steel Stairs															E	LL	L	
230	4	49																
Steel Framing and Pan Forms													EE	LL				
300	5	22																
Steel Exterior Stairs														E	L			
303	1	43																
Place Concrete														EEEE	LLLL			
305	16	0																
Steel Studs															EEE			LL
310	8	6																

160

Interior Spiral Steel Stairs
330   4   40

Steel Framing and Pan Forms
400   5   33

Steel Exterior Stairs
403   1   52

Place Concrete
405   16   0

Steel Studs
410   8   4

Interior Spiral Steel Stairs
430   4   31

Steel Framing and Pan Forms
500   5   44

Steel Exterior stairs
503   1   61

Place Concrete
505   16   0

Steel Studs
510   8   2

Interior Spiral Steel Stairs
530   4   22

Steel Framing and Pan Forms
600   5   55

Steel Exterior Stairs
603   1   70

Place Concrete
605   16   0

Steel Studs
610   8   0

Interior Spiral Steel Stairs
630   4   13

161

developing alternative plans for changing schedules based on limited resources. There are two types of features that scheduling software can provide. In Primavera, for example, these are called resource leveling and resource constraining. Leveling allocates workers, without effecting the duration of the schedule, by "sliding" from a schedule based on an early start of all activities to a schedule that shows some activities starting at a later date. Resource-constraining limits the use of a resource to a user-specified level, and actually modifies the project's duration as necessary.

The algorithms used for resource leveling and constraining in scheduling systems may be significantly different, although they all follow the same general procedure. The first step is to choose an activity that needs the limited resource. This activity is then scheduled. The remaining amount of the resource will then be evaluated to determine whether other activities can be scheduled concurrently. The process is repeated until all activities have been scheduled. The key to these algorithms is the order in which activities are chosen to be scheduled. There are many different varieties. Some of the ways to choose activities are First In-First Out (also called FIFO), total float, and late start.

The usefulness of resource leveling and constraint algorithms, in most scheduling software, is limited in large construction projects. The complexity of the algorithms that automatically reschedule activity start and finish dates makes the analysis of the revised schedule difficult. The scheduler will want to know why the scheduling system modified the schedule dates. In order to determine why schedule dates have been moved, the scheduler will have to perform detailed analysis to determine why activities have been shifted. Until the scheduler becomes very familiar with the way that the scheduling system's resource algorithms function, the scheduler will not be able to use the methods satisfactorily on large construction projects.

ALTERNATIVE RESOURCE ANALYSIS METHODS

Since resource analysis is very cumbersome, using the traditional analysis, construction management researchers and practitioners have proposed several other methods. Two of these methods, the fenced bar chart[5] and the Vertical Production Method[6] (VPM) are described in this section. Both of these methods are useful only if there is a significant number of repetitive elements in the construction project.

The fenced bar chart combines the advantage of the intuitive understandability of a bar chart and the logic of the critical path method schedule. Activities are shown as bars banded according to crew type. The critical logic between bands of activities are shown on the graph as lines, or "fences." These fences mark the limits within which a set of activities may float without impacting on other crews or the critical path.

The second alternative to using CPM software to assist in resource analysis is to use the Vertical Production Method (VPM) shown in Figure 6.8. The VPM, like the fenced bar chart, is also a graphical approach to showing crew chases through a project. In order to produce a VPM diagram, the scheduler begins by placing a time line across the bottom of a page (the X-axis), and a scale representing the percent complete of an activity along the left side of the page (the Y-axis). The scheduler then plots when various sets of activities with similar work will start on the project and when the series of activities may be completed. In VPM, all of the concrete slab activities appear on the "Place Concrete" line. The Place Concrete line illustrates that this crew arrives on the site on day zero, completes work up to the fourth floor after 64 working days, and completes all of the work on the 96th day after arriving on-site.

To use VPM, activities for the installation of metal stud walls will now be added to the graph. Figure 6.9 shows the progression of the two sets of activities, concrete slabs and stud wall installation, used in the crew design section of this chapter. If an attempt to schedule the stud installation using the early start date is made, a diagram showing the split solution illustrated previously is generated. The

---

[5]Melin, John W. and Whiteaker, Barry, "Fencing a Bar Chart," American Society of Civil Engineers, *Journal of the Construction Division*, Vol. 103, No. CO3., Sept 1981. pp. 497–507.
[6]O'Brien, James J., "VPM Scheduling for High-Rise Buildings," American Society of Civil Engineers, *Journal of the Construction Division*, Vol. 101, No. CO4, December 1975, pp. 895–904. See also Johnston, David W., "Linear Scheduling Method for Highway Construction", *Journal of the Construction Division*, Vol 107, No. CO2, June 1981. pp. 247–261. VPM is also referred to as Line-of-Balance.

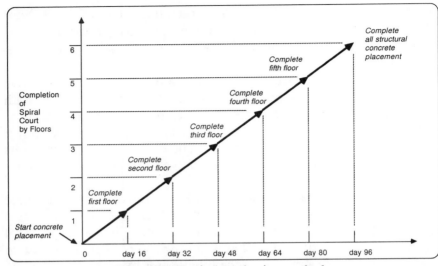

Figure 6.8. Vertical production method.

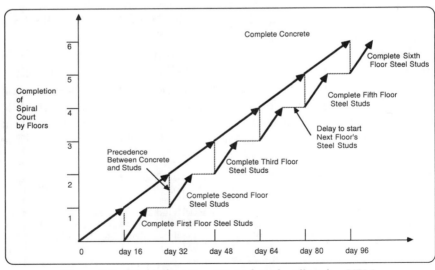

Figure 6.9. Scheduling concrete and stud walls using VPM.

vertical line from the end of the first concrete placement activity to the beginning of the first stud wall activity shows the logic of the work reflected in a CPM analysis. The VPM diagram clearly illustrates that there is a period when the steel crew is inactive and should be pulled off of the site.

Developing the proper crew chase through the network is accomplished by delaying the start of the steel stud wall installation until day 56, as shown in Figure 6.10. This approach provides the efficient, nonsplit, solution for the taping and finishing crew. The VPM can be used to develop proper crew chases for the project, and the data may be fed back to the CPM schedule for project monitoring and control.

What actually occurs on most projects occurs somewhere between the split and nonsplit schedule. The slope of each line represents the productivity of each crew. If the carpentry crew arrives on the construction site to begin work on day 16, then Figure 6.9 shows that the crew will have approximately 8 days of idle time before beginning the second set of taping work. This ideal time is usually taken up by a reduction in productivity by workers. Figure 6.11 illustrates the effect of reduced productivity on the first steel stud wall activity. Since the production rate has decreased, the metal stud

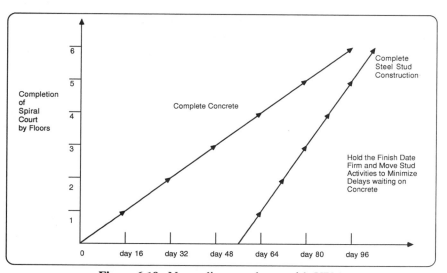

Figure 6.10. Non-split crew chases with VPM.

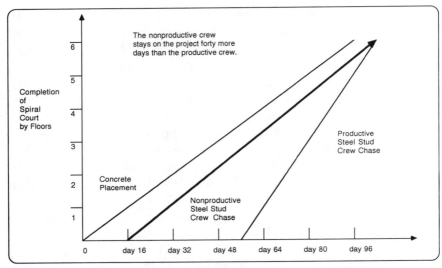

Figure 6.11. Showing productivity losses using VPM.

wall construction may now be accomplished in sequence. Figure 6.11 illustrates that forty nonproductive crew days may be saved by using the nonsplit solution.

The adage that a project will expand to fit the time available is clearly evident in Figure 6.11. Although developing a proper crew design is a difficult process, whether using the CPM, a fenced bar chart, or the VPM, the common result of this effort is projects that run within cost and an increased contractor's profit margin.

Part 3
The Future of Scheduling Software

Chapter 7

Current Research

INTRODUCTION

Software vendors have worked very hard to make CPM technology accessible to a wide audience. Even the most sophisticated scheduling software for desktop computers is available at a total hardware and software cost of under $5000. The interaction between the user and these programs has become very sophisticated. For smaller projects, interactive graphics are a very powerful tool. For larger projects, menu systems and data entry screens may be customized as required by the needs of the project.

Two fundamental problems that plague the original mainframe versions of CPM, however, still remain in the best microcomputer scheduling programs. The first problem is that the systems must be fed large amounts of data to remain current. The second is that the volume of output provided from the programs often keeps even experienced schedulers from conducting a rigorous schedule analysis. Thus, microcomputer programs allow the construction office to work faster, but not necessarily smarter.

This chapter provides a brief survey of efforts to enhance contemporary scheduling systems. Next, ways to extend scheduling software will be discussed, using traditional programming techniques. Applications of artificial intelligence to construction planning will then be briefly described.

In Chapter Five, several schedule analysis questions were answered, using scheduling reports, which supported sorting and selecting activities. There are, however, many questions that can not be answered by just sorting and selecting via activity codes. One such question is "Is the construction progress sufficient to allow the project to be completed on time?" While several project management systems provide "target" reporting capabilities, these do not fully support progress analysis.

Target reports compare schedules in order to inform the user of changes in each current activity's float, as compared to earlier schedules. Other types of comparison reports show the differences between the expected earnings and actual earnings in the form of "S-curves," shown in Figure 6.1. Although these curves can be used effectively to determine the impact of previous poor performance, they do not analyze this impact and prepare revised schedules based upon future activities that may be delayed in similar ways. This problem is illustrated in Figure 6.2.

A better way to identify trends in construction progress is by following these steps: (1) Search all previous schedules to see whether the actual activity duration was greater or less than the originally scheduled duration; (2) Identify all activities that were delayed, and attempt to discover a pattern to explain the delay; (3) Adjust all future activities that are likely to be delayed; and (4) Recalculate the schedule in light of the new schedule data. Once the above steps have been followed, the results of the changes can be evaluated. The steps required to answer other critical questions, such as "Can the project be built as shown in the construction plan?" and "Will this project be profitable?" are even more intricate, using existing scheduling software. Construction management researchers are currently developing a new generation of scheduling software that will incorporate features to answer these and other difficult questions.

SPECIALIZED NETWORK ANALYSIS TOOLS

The need for project managers to monitor variances between planned and actual completion is well known to software vendors. Although some systems provide variance analysis using target reports, there are new products available that represent dramatic steps toward trend analysis.

Parade (Primavera Systems) compares versions of schedules and prepares both cost and time variances, based on the original planned schedule versus subsequent schedule updates. One interesting feature of this system is that, in addition to viewing trends in cost and time thresholds for variances, it may also be used to provide "automatic" reporting.

Variances are identified at a multileveled work breakdown structure, similar to the Construction Specification Index. Variances may also be broken out by other codes, including Responsibility. Although Parade represents a step towards automating schedule analysis, the amount of data produced by the Parade system creates additional data analysis burdens. Another drawback to the Parade system is that it utilizes proprietary data formats.

Another system for automated schedule analysis utilizes dBase III+[1] programming to analyze schedule data. This system is called the PROject MANagement system, or PROMAN. PROMAN was developed by the authors for use on large projects undertaken by the U.S. Army Corps of Engineers. PROMAN provides a number of analysis tools, including: the integration of submittal and schedule data; a detailed comparison of schedule versions; an as-planned variance analysis for cost, time, and resource loading; an analysis of float depletion; a trace and analysis of the critical path; trend analysis for up to five previous schedules; and an activity code checker.

Analysis tools like those present in PROMAN may be quickly developed by construction offices. The tools that may be developed fall into two general categories: data preprocessors and postprocessors.

One example of a preprocessor is an activity code assistant. This analysis tool takes an activity description and provides suggested activity codes based on activity coding databases. Each activity coding database contains sets of words, and their synonyms, that correspond to a single activity code. As an activity description is evaluated, the codes corresponding to that description are suggested to the user. The activity coding checker should not make all of the decisions for the scheduler, since evaluating activity descriptions by using database techniques may not always provide one precise set of codes. For example, activity descriptions that contain "steel," "structural steel," or "steel studs" should have different coding schemes. The activity code checker should suggest all of the potential codes and allow the user to select the one that is most appropriate. A database of project-specific synonyms and abbreviations may also be created to support particular projects.

---

[1] dBase III+ is a registered trademark of Ashton Tate Corporation.

One set of postprocessing tools that can benefit many offices compares submittal and procurement systems with schedule activity data. One possible report created from the use of this type of tool lists all activity numbers, with the submittals that pertain to a particular activity listed below it. Another report shows those submittals without a valid activity number. These first two reports may be used to verify that the submittal and schedule systems are fully compatible. The next report lists any schedule activities that will be delayed, based on the submittal item delivery dates. These delays are identified in a manner similar to how a project manager might review delays. The activity delays that are the most critical are those on and within two weeks of the critical path. Delayed activities with a float greater than two weeks will only be noted if the delay is large compared to the amount of float. For example, if an activity had 40 working days of float and was delayed by a late material delivery by 2 days, then the activity will not appear on the report.

One way to think of these types of reports is as "data filters." Reports that provide a "filtering" capability dramatically decrease the amount of raw data that schedule postprocessing reports produce and significantly increase the project manager's ability to rapidly identify critical data.

Another set of postprocessing reports that can be rapidly developed in the construction office enable a review of the differences in time, cost, and resources among similar activities. A simple statistical program determines the mean and standard deviations of schedule data, according to a user-specified activity code, such as Subcontractor or Building Systems Index. The results of such a report, which lists those activities that are within a user-defined number of standard deviations above or below the mean, can be printed out for analysis. This report assists the reviewer in determining the consistency of the schedule, and indicates whether the schedule data is skewed in a particular area.

One of the most time-consuming tasks for the scheduler is tracing through a network to identify activities on the critical (or some other) path, and discovering the way in which these activities are related. Two types of reports may be developed for this type of analysis. The first report addresses the time required to trace through schedule paths. Tracing paths is time-consuming because activity data is usually transferred from an activity logic report, in

PDM, or an *i-j* sort, for ADM, to another report that only shows activities in the path of interest. This programming effort would perform the tracing and produce a report that shows a user-defined number of the most critical paths through the schedule. Each path is then analyzed for activities with large durations, few allocated man-hours, or long lag times. The analysis provides a rapid method of identifying ways to decrease the duration of the critical path. The second type of report could address the time required to identify, and then verify, the patterns of repetitive activities being used throughout the network. This report selects a user-defined set of activities, according to Work Area and Building Systems Index (BSI), and then lists their succeeding activities. This report, once completed for several Work Areas, quickly shows whether repetitive logic is being used throughout the project.

Slippage of various types of activities may also be identified with database programming techniques. These schedule postprocessing tools would identify categories of activities whose "original" versus "actual" activity duration have changed significantly during the entire history of the project.

A final set of postprocessing programs could allow a scheduler to easily compare all changes between any two schedules. Although many commercially available scheduling systems provide schedule comparison reports, these reports are not designed for a periodic audit of all schedule changes. This detailed audit is the only way to have full confidence in schedule updates.

Whether using commercially available add-on schedule postprocessors or developing custom applications for use with local system configurations, the effort spent will be immediately rewarded in both tangible and intangible returns. One of the most tangible benefits is that more detailed schedule analysis can be consistently performed at the construction office. The time required to perform schedule analysis will also be reduced. An intangible benefit is an increased management confidence in schedule data, because changes are clearly trailed.

AI AND SCHEDULING

A branch of computer science known as Artificial Intelligence (AI) appears to hold the promise to allow project managers to do their jobs in new ways.[2] One goal of AI is to develop "intelligent" programs.[3] AI covers a wide variety of topics, including vision, machine learning, natural language understanding, planning, robotics, and expert systems.[4] Although the field of AI is quite broad, it is not necessary for a user or even for a systems developer to understand how the mind works or even to simulate human behavior in order to reap significant commercial benefits by applying AI technology today.[5]

Since many readers may be unfamiliar with AI terminology, we will provide a brief introduction to a few AI issues appropriate to schedule analysis. There are many excellent papers and books that describe the AI field and its application to project planning. The reader is encouraged to refer to the references cited throughout this section for a more thorough presentation.

The expert system area of AI has gained more attention in the past several years than other areas of AI, due to the potential of developing commercial systems. The term "expert system" (or knowledge-based system) is often used to loosely describe many types of systems that incorporate knowledge regarding a specific, narrow range of topics. Expert systems were developed to simulate a consulting session that a novice might have with an expert in a particular field or "domain."

Over two-thirds of the Fortune 500 companies are currently developing expert system applications. The total AI market is projected to grow from $1 billion in 1986 to over $4 billion in 1990. Some examples of expert system in use today are: approving authorizations for credit card purchases, financial planning, planning the

[2]Levitt, Raymond E. and Kunz, John C., Using artificial intelligence techniques to support project management. *AI EDAM*, Vol. 1, No. 1, Feb. 1987. pp. 3–24.
[3]Winston, Patrick Henry, *Artificial Intelligence*, 2nd ed. Reading, MA: Addison-Wesley Publishing, p. 1.
[4]For further information see Schank, Roger C. What is AI, anyway? *AI Magazine*, Vol. 8, No. 4, December 1987. pp. 57–66, and Kurzweil, Raymond. What is artificial intellegence anyway? *American Scientist*, Vol. 73, pp. 258–264.
[5]For several examples of operational AI systems, the reader should refer to Davis, Dwight B. Artificial intelligence goes to work, *High Technology*, April 1987. pp. 16–27; and Oxman, Steven W., *An Executive Report on Expert Systems, Use in Support of Management Decision Making*. Netherlands: Oxko Publications, 1984. pp. 14–19.

manufacture of aircraft components, determining computer configurations, and diagnosing problems with robots.[6]

The most important difference between traditional programming
and expert systems is that knowledge is not translated into difficult-
to-understand computer programming languages. Instead, it is represented symbolically, using English-like grammar and syntax.
Since effective representation of knowledge is one of the most important issues in AI system development, the next three sections will
briefly discuss the three most frequently used knowledge representa-
tions; rules, frames, and object-oriented programming.

An example of a rule that may be used in a schedule analysis
program is, "If an activity uses concrete and it is winter, then there
must be a weather-protection activity." To execute this rule, the
inference engine finds every activity that uses concrete, selects those
activities that are scheduled in the winter, and then finds any
weather-protection activities and selects those which happen at the
same time as the concrete activity. If weather protection is included
in the schedule, then the system provides that information. If no
weather-protection activities are found, the system would tell the
user that there could be a problem with placing concrete during the
bad weather period.

Since there are many rules that need to be included in an expert
system for schedule analysis, the "inference engine" must determine
the order in which the rules will "fire" and provide the appropriate
information to the user.[7] A paper in the American Society of Civil
Engineers' book, *Expert Systems in Civil Engineering*, describes a
rule-based system for schedule analysis.

Frame-based systems enhance the "packaging" of data and
knowledge about an item of interest by creating a special type of
data structure, called a "frame."[8] Once the available facts are obtained, the frame-based system uses rules to draw conclusions. A
frame for a "Clear and Grub" activity is contained in Table 7.1.

---

[6]ibid, Davis, 1987 and Oxman, 1984.
[7]O'Connor, Michael J. DeLaGarza, Jesus M., and Ibbs, C. William. In *An Expert System for
Construction Schedule Analysis*. Kortem and Maher, eds. ASCE, 1987.
[8]One good work on frame-based systems is: Fikes, Richard, and Kehler, Tom. The role of
frame-based representation in reasoning. *Communications of the ACM*, Vol. 28, No. 9, Sept
85. pp. 904–920.

Table 7.1. Simplified activity frame.

FRAME_NAME:	Clear_and_Grub
PARENT_FRAME:	Site_Work
ACTIVITY_ID:	1000
DURATION:	20
ACTUAL_START:	01Oct88
ACTUAL_FINISH:	
PERCENT_COMPLETE:	50
AFFECTED_BY:	

While a single frame appears to be quite like a database record, the frame structure also allows an individual frame to be part of a tree-like hierarchy of other frames. The example frame "Clear_and_Grub" might, therefore, be attached to another frame called "Site_Work." This "parent" frame, "Site_Work," may also have other "child" frames for "Grading" and "Landscaping." The example frame "Site_Work" is shown in Table 7.2. Notice that this frame does not need to have the same information as its child "Clear_and_Grub."

The real power of this hierarchical frame structure lies in a feature called "inheritance." Inheritance allows the child frames to extract unknown information from its parent frame(s). For example, if one wanted to determine whether the "Clear_and_Grub" activity would be affected by any type of weather, the program would first look in the AFFECTED_BY slot of the "Clear_and_Grub" activity. Since no value is present, the program then looks in the AFFECTED_BY slot of the PARENT_FRAME, "Site_Work," and gets the value of "precipitation."

Object-oriented programming uses frames and rules in a more "opportunistic" way. In object-oriented programming, slots may contain procedure names, which are executed when the procedure's conditions are met. These procedures, often called "demons," pass

Table 7.2. Parent frame.

FRAME_NAME:	Site_Work
PARENT_FRAME:	Project_X
CHILD_FRAMES:	Clear_and_Grub, Grading, Landscaping
AFFECTED_BY:	precipitation

"messages," or new values, to other slots in the frame or to other frames. Thus, object-oriented programming tends to consolidate all knowledge about a frame directly inside the frame. The knowledge is used as needed as the system runs.

An example of how object-oriented programming might be used is in the calculation of activity completion dates. Once the start date of an activity has been entered, the demon would add the duration of the activity to the start date and place this new finish date in the activity's completion date slot. The power of the object-oriented system is that schedule data and knowledge may contain not only data, but also procedures that govern its use. Since these systems allow demons to be identified by slot values, the demons, like any other type of value, may be inherited from parent frames. A paper by Levitt and Kunz describes one application of object-oriented programming for updating construction plans.[9]

Developing a knowledge-based system may take as little as a few months or as long as five or six years.[10] While large systems that cover a broad area of application may take several years to complete, even small systems that take little time to create may produce large cost savings. The paper by Dym[11] addresses some very important issues in the design and construction of knowledge-based systems.

[9]Levitt, Raymond E. and Kunz, John C. Using knowledge of construction and project management for automated schedule updating. *Project Management Journal*, Vol. XIV, No. 5, December 1985. pp. 57–76.
[10]Buchannan, Bruce G. and Smith, Reid. Expert systems project management. *Tutorial Session MA2*, American Association of Artificial Intelligence. July 13, 1987.
[11]Dym, Clive L. Issues in the design and implementation of expert systems. *AI EDAM*, Vol. 1, No. 1, 1987. pp. 3–24.

Chapter 8

Gazing into the Crystal Ball

The scheduling software of the next century must provide additional pre- and postprocessing assistance. These systems should interact with a user, who may not be familiar with more than the basics of CPM, to build a detailed project or construction schedule. To accomplish this, the systems will need to have substantial built-in knowledge, in order to create, review, and adjust the network developed. The need for real-time responses, and the amount of knowledge required to provide this assistance, will eventually force the development of a new generation of scheduling software.

These new systems will initially create a schedule using knowledge about construction and a historical data base of projects. Once the system creates the initial schedule, multiwindow graphical interfaces will allow the user to interact with the system and make the necessary changes for a particular project setting.

Once the schedule is constructed, the plan will be updated by using automated data acquisition systems. These data acquisition systems could include hand-held devices, such as bar code readers, and automated analysis of job progress video tapes. During the progress of the job, intelligent alarms will point out potential difficulties and suggest possible changes.

During schedule reviews, such systems will assist in the process by identifying delayed activities. These systems could also be developed to make "educated" guesses regarding the cause of delay.

Scheduling systems of the future will offer a wide range of intelligent features. Although the basics of scheduling will always need to be known by humans, in order to operate these systems, the mechanisms for creating and analyzing detailed networks will be the responsibility of computers. Some analysts have said that leaving schedule generation, updating, and analysis to computers will reduce the need for specialists, a theory with which we disagree. The reason for using tools, whether it be a power screwdriver or a microchip, is to free the knowledgeable individual to perform more effectively. As scheduling software moves into the twenty-first century, intelligent tools will become the specialist's partner, to insure that projects are completed on time and within budget.

Appendix A1

Data Exchange Specifications

7 Nov 89

SPECIAL CONTRACT CLAUSE: CONTRACTOR PREPARED NETWORK ANALYSIS SYSTEM (NAS)

(a) General:

The progress chart to be prepared by the Contractor pursuant to the Contract Clause, "SCHEDULE FOR CONSTRUCTION CONTRACTS" shall consist of a network analysis system (NAS) as described below. The scheduling of construction is the responsibility of the Contractor and Contractor management personnel shall actively participate in its development. The purpose of the NAS is to verify that the Contractor's plan meets contract requirements and to determine if the construction plan is reasonable and will allow the contractor to complete the project within the contract duration. During construction the approved NAS will be used to measure the progress of the work and to aid in evaluating time extensions.

(b) Required Personnel Qualifications:

The Contractor shall designate an authorized representative who shall be responsible for the preparation of all required NAS reports. This person shall have previously created and reviewed computerized schedules. Qualifications of this individual shall be submitted to the Contracting Officer for approval with the Preliminary NAS submission (see Paragraph d, this section).

(c) Network Analysis System (NAS) Description:

The Network Analysis System (NAS) shall consist of network diagrams, required reports, and a data disk required by Technical Specification 01013, "Data Exchange Format." The automated scheduling system utilized by the Contractor shall be capable of providing all requirements of this specification.

1. Use of the Critical Path Method:

The Critical Path Method (CPM) of network calculation shall be used to generate the NAS. The Contractor shall provide the NAS in either Arrow Diagram Method (ADM) or Precedence Format (PDM) as described in the Critical Path Method (CPM) of network calculations. U.S. Army Corps of Engineers Engineering Pamphlet 415-1-4, "Network Analysis Systems," provides a basic introduction to NAS and CPM.

2. Level of Detail Required:

With the exception of the preliminary schedule submission, the NAS shall include an appropriate level of detail. The Contracting Officer shall use, but is not limited to, the following conditions to review compliance with this paragraph:

a. The submittal, review, procurement, fabrication, delivery, installation, start-up, and testing of special or long lead materials and equipment shall be included in the NAS. Long lead materials are those materials that have a procurement cycle of over ninety (90) days.

b. Owner and other agencies activities that could impact progress shall be shown. These activities include, but are not limited to: approvals, inspections, utility tie-in, Owner furnished equipment and notice to proceed for phasing requirements.

c. Less than two percent (2%) of all non-procurement activities' Original Durations shall be greater than 20 days.

d. Only one type of work crew in a single work area shall be grouped to form an activity.

3. Contract, Phased Completion Time.

The schedule interval shall extend from notice-to-proceed to contract completion date that is specified in the "COMMENCEMENT PROSECUTION AND COMPLETION OF WORK" Special Clause. The schedule shall start no earlier than the date that the Notice to Proceed was Acknowledged. Completion of the last activity in the schedule shall be constrained by the contract completion date. This constraint shall be such that if the late finish of the last activity falls after the contract completion date, then the float calculation shall reflect a negative float on the critical path. Contractually, specified interim dates shall also be constrained as appropriate.

4. Use of Scheduling System Default Dates:

NAS data shall not be automatically updated by default dates contained in many CPM scheduling software systems. This includes, but is not limited to, the automatic assignment of either: (a) Remaining Durations or Percent Complete, (b) Actual Start or Actual Finish Dates. Activities that have posted progress without predecessors and activities being completed (Out-of-Sequence Progress) shall be allowed only by the case-by-case approval of the Contracting Officer's Representative. The Contracting Officer's Representative may direct that changes in schedule logic be made to correct any or all out-of-sequence work.

(d) Preliminary NAS Submission:

A Preliminary NAS network diagram, defining the Contractors planned operations for the first 60 days shall be submitted for approval within (20) calendar days after notice to proceed is acknowledged. The approved preliminary schedule shall be used for payment purposes not to exceed 60 calendar days after notice to proceed. Approval of the preliminary, and subsequent NAS submissions shall be contingent upon approval of the Contractor's choice of authorized scheduling representative.

(e) Initial NAS Submission:

The Initial NAS shall be submitted for approval within (40) calendar days after notice to proceed. The initial NAS shall provide (1) a reasonable sequence of activities through the entire project and (2) the specified level of activity detail (see Paragraph c.2.) Progress payments shall be withheld by the contracting officer until the contractor submits an acceptable schedule in the proper electronic data exchange medium. Retainage up to the maximum allowed by contract may be withheld at each payment period until corrections to the NAS have been approved.

(f) Progress Meetings:

Progress meetings to discuss payment, shall include a monthly on-site meeting or other regular intervals mutually agreed to at the preconstruction conference. During this meeting the Contractor will describe, on an activity by activity basis, all proposed revisions and adjustments to the NAS required to reflect the current status of the project. The Contracting Officer shall approve activity progress, proposed revisions, and adjustments as appropriate.

1. Meeting Attendance.

At a minimum, the Contractor's Project Manager and Scheduler shall attend the regular progress meeting.

2. Update Submission Following Progress Meeting.

A complete update of the NAS containing all approved progress, revisions, and adjustments, based on the regular progress meeting, shall be submitted not later than four (4) working days after the monthly progress meeting.

3. Progress Meeting Contents:

Update information, i.e. Actual Start Dates, Actual Finish Dates, Remaining Durations, and Cost to Date shall be subject to the approval of the Contracting Officer's Representative. The following is a minimum set of items which the Contractor shall address, on an activity by activity basis, during each progress meeting:

a. The Actual Start and Actual Finish dates of each activity currently in-progress or completed activities.

b. The estimated Remaining Duration for each activity in-progress. Time-Based progress calculations must be based on Remaining Duration for each activity.

c. The Cost to Date for each activity started. Payment shall be based on Cost to Date for each in-progress or completed activity.

d. All logic changes pertaining to "Notice to Proceed" on change orders, change orders to be incorporated into the network, and contractor proposed changes in activity sequence, corrections to schedule logic for out-of-sequence progress, and durations which have been made pursuant to contract provisions shall be discussed.

e. All changes required due to delays in completion of any activity or group of activities. Included in these requirements are those delays beyond the Contractors control such as strikes, unusual weather. Also included are delays encountered due to submittals, Government Activities, deliveries or work stoppage which makes replanning the work necessary and when the schedule does not represent the actual prosecution and progress of the work.

(g) NAS Submission Reporting:

The Contractor shall submit (1) two sets of disks which follow electronic data format specified, (2) three (3) copies of the specified reports, and (3) three (3) copies of the network diagram. The Contractor shall provide this information for the Preliminary, Initial, and every Monthly NAS update throughout the life of the project. Failure to submit the complete submission as described in this paragraph shall result in disapproval of the entire submission:

1. Data Disk Requirement:

As many data disk(s) as required, in the "Standard Data Exchange Format," shall be provided with the Preliminary, Initial, Monthly Updates, and all NAS revisions or request for revision. Refer to Technical Specifications Section 01013 for complete description of this format.

2. Narrative Report:

a. Construction Progress Narrative:

A Narrative Report shall be provided with each update of the NAS. This report shall be provided as the basis of the Contractor's progress payment request. The Narrative Report shall include: (1) a description of activities along the four most critical paths, (2) a description of current and anticipated problem areas or delaying factors and their impact, and (3) an explanation of corrective actions taken.

b. Approved Changes Verification:

Only NAS changes that have been previously approved by the Contracting Officer shall be included in the schedule submission. The Narrative Report shall specifically reference, on an activity by activity basis, all changes made since the previous period and relate each change to documented, approved schedule changes.

3. Logic Report:

a. Content:

The Activity and Logic Report shall be a listing of all activities sorted according to activity number. Activities shall be printed in ascending order.

b. Format:

The printed report shall contain: Activity Number(s), Activity Description, Original Duration, Remaining Duration, Early Start Date, Early Finish Date, Late Start Date, Late Finish Date, Total Float. For Precedence schedules Preceding and Succeeding activities for each activity shall be printed.

4. Criticality Report:

a. Content:

The Criticality Report shall be a listing of all activities sorted in ascending order of total float. Activities which have the same amount of total float shall be listed in ascending order of Early Start Dates.

b. Format:

The printed report shall contain: Activity Number(s), Activity Description, Original Duration, Remaining Duration, Early Start Date, Early Finish Date, Late Start Date, Late Finish Date, Total Float.

5. Earned Value Report:

a. Content:

The Earned Value Report shall compile the Contractor's total Earned Value on the project from the Notice to Proceed until the most recent Monthly Progress Meeting. This report shall reflect the Earned Value of specific activities based on the agreements made in the field and approved between the Contractor and Contracting Officer at the most recent Monthly Progress Meeting. Provided that the Contractor has provided a complete schedule update, this report shall serve as the basis of determining Contractor Payment.

b. Format:

Activities shall be grouped by bid item and then sorted by activity number(s). This report shall: (1) sum all activities in a bid item and provide a bid item percent complete and (2) sum all bid items to provide a total project percent complete. The printed report shall contain, for each activity: Activity Number(s), Activity Description, Original Duration, Remaining Duration, Early Start Date, Early Finish Date, Late Start Date, Late Finish Date, Total Float, Estimated Earned Value, Percent Complete (based on cost), Earnings to Date.

6. User Defined Reports: (included by U.S. Army Corps of Engineers Construction Field Office)

a. Contents: (included by Corps Field Office)

b. Format: (included by Corps Field Office)

7. Network Diagram Requirements:

Network Diagrams shall depict and display the order and interdependence of activities and the sequence in which the work is to be accomplished. The network diagram shall only be required for initial schedule submission. The Contracting Officer shall use, but is not limited to, the following conditions to review compliance with this paragraph:

a. Diagrams shall be drafted to show a continuous flow from left to right with no arrows from right to left. The activity number, description and duration shall be shown on the diagram.

b. Dates shall be shown on the diagram for start of project, any contract required milestones, and contract completion dates.

c. The critical path shall be clearly marked.

d. Activities may be grouped according to either building area or types of work crews, as directed by the Contracting Officer.

(h) Payment Based on NAS Updates:

The Contractor shall be entitled to progress payments determined from the currently approved NAS update. If the Contractor fails or refuses to furnish the information and NAS Data, which in the judgment of the Contracting Officer, is necessary for verifying the Contractor's progress, the Contractor shall be deemed not to have provided an estimate upon which progress payment may be made.

(i) Justification of Contractor's Request For Time.

In the event the Contractor requests an extension of the contract completion date, he shall furnish such justification, NAS data and supporting evidence as the Contracting Officer may deem necessary for a determination as to whether or not the Contractor is entitled to an extension of time under the provisions of the contract. Submission of proof of delay, based on revised activity logic, duration, and costs (updated to the specific date that the delay occurred) is obligatory to any approvals.

1. Justification of Delay:

The schedule must clearly display that the Contractor has used, in full, all the float time available for the work involved with this request. The Contracting Officer's determination as to the number of allowable days of contract extension, shall be based upon the NAS schedule updates in effect for the time period in question and other factual information. Actual delays that are found to be caused by the contractor's own actions, which result in the extension of the predicted contract completion dates, according to the schedule, shall not be a cause for a time extension to the contract completion date.

2. Submission Requirements:

The Contractor shall submit a justification for each request for a change in the contract completion date of under two weeks based upon the most recent schedule update at the time of the Notice to Proceed or constructive direction issued for the change. Such a request shall be in accordance with the requirements of other appropriate Contract Clauses and shall include, as a minimum: (1) a list of affected activities, with their associated NAS activity number, (2) a brief explanation of the causes of the change, (3) an analysis of the overall impact of the changes proposed, and (4) a sub-network of the affected area.

3. Additional Submission Requirements:

For any request for time extension for over two (2) weeks, the Contracting Officer may request an interim update with revised activities for a specific change request. The Contractor shall provide this disk within four (4) days of the Contracting Officer's request.

(j) Ownership of Float.

Float available in the schedule, at any time, shall not be considered for the exclusive use of either the Government, the owner, or the Contractor.

End of Section

Appendix A2

Draft Guide Specification

Technical Specification 01013— Mar 90
SCHEDULING SYSTEM DATA EXCHANGE FORMAT

PART 1—GENERAL

1. Application of this Provision:

The data exchange format provides a platform for exchanging scheduling and planning data between various software systems. This section shall be used in conjunction with the Special Contract Clause, SC-20, entitled, "Contractor— PREPARED NETWORK ANALYSIS SYSTEM." The Data Exchange Format shall allow project management systems to share information with other programs. Scheduling information shall be transferred from the Contractors project management system to the Government as described in this section.

2. Electronic Data Exchange File Required for All Schedule Submissions:

   a. The Contractor shall provide schedule data in the Data Exchange Format for each Preliminary, Initial, Monthly NAS Updates, and requests for time extensions or change proposals. The Contractor's failure to provide schedule data in the exact format described, herein, shall result in disapproval of the entire schedule submission.

   b. The entire set of schedule data shall be transferred at every exchange of scheduling data. Thus, for updates to existing projects, the data exchange file shall contain all activities that have not started or are already complete as well as those activities in progress.

3. Data Transfer Responsibility:

The Contractor shall be responsible for Electronic Data Exchange File data that may have been lost or destroyed during transit between the Contractor and the Contracting Officer. If Electronic Data Exchange File data is damaged during transit, then the Contractor shall provide the Contracting Officer with a new Electronic Data Exchange File within two (2) working days of notification by the Contracting Officer.

4. Data Consistency Responsibility:

The Contractor shall be responsible for the consistency between the Electronic Data Exchange File and printed reports which accompany schedule submissions. If Electronic Data Exchange File data for a schedule submission differs, in any way, from the printed schedule reports or standard activity coding, then the Contracting Officer shall disapprove the entire schedule submission. The Contractor shall provide the Contracting Officer with a completely revised, and consistent, schedule submission within 24 hours of notification of inconsistency by the Contracting Officer.

5. Creating the Electronic Data Exchange File:

The Contractor shall have the option of creating the electronic data exchange file by one of the three following methods:

a. Commercially Available Software:

The Contractor shall be required to secure software that meets this requirement. Many commercially available scheduling systems support the standard data exchange format.

b. Interface Program:

Under this option the Contractor shall produce their own data translation software. This software shall take the information provided by the Contractor's scheduling system and reformat the data into the Data Exchange Format.

c. Manual Methods:

Under this option the Contractor shall manually reformat the Contractor's scheduling system report files or create all necessary data by manually entering all data into the Data Exchange Format.

PART 2—GENERAL DATA EXCHANGE FILE REQUIREMENTS

6. File Transfer Medium:

All required data shall be submitted on a minimum of 5¼" diskette(s), formatted to hold 360 KB of data, under the MS-DOS version 2.0 (or greater) operating system. Higher data densities and other operating systems may be approved by the Contracting Officer if compatible with the owner's computing capability.

7. File Type and Format:

The data file shall consist of a 132 character, fixed format, "ASCII" file. Text shall be left-justified and numbers shall be right-justified in each field. Data records must conform, exactly, to the sequence, column position, maximum length, mandatory values, and field definitions described below to comply with this standard data exchange format. Unless specifically stated, all numbers shall be whole numbers. All data columns shall be separated by a single blank column.

8. Electronic Data Exchange File Name:

The Contractor shall insure that each file has a name related to either the schedule data date, project name, or contract number. No two Electronic Data Exchange Files shall have the same name throughout the life of this contract. The Contractor shall submit their file naming convention to the Contracting Officer for Approval. In the event that the Contractor's naming convention is Disapproved, the Contracting Officer shall direct the Contractor to provide files under a unique file naming convention.

9. Disk Label:

The Contractor shall affix a permanent exterior label to each diskette submitted. The label shall contain the type of schedule (Preliminary, Initial, Update or Change), full project number, project name, project location, data date, name and telephone number of Contractors Scheduler, and MS-DOS version used to format the diskette.

10. Standard Activity Coding Dictionary:

The Contractor shall submit, with the initial schedule submission, a consistent coding scheme that shall be used throughout the project for the Activity Codes shown in Paragraph 12.e of this section. The coding scheme submitted shall demonstrate that each code only represents one type of information through the duration of the contract. Incomplete coding of activities or an incomplete coding scheme shall be sufficient for disapproval of the schedule.

PART 3—DATA FORMAT

11. Data Exchange File Format Organization:

The Data Exchange File Format shall consist of the following records provided in the exact sequence shown below:

Paragraph Reference	Record Description	Remarks
12.a	VOLUME RECORD	First Record on Every Data Disk
12.b	PROJECT RECORD	Second Record on First Data Disk
12.c	CALENDAR RECORD(S)	Minimum of One Record Required
12.d	HOLIDAY RECORD(S)	Optional Record
12.e	ACTIVITY RECORD(S)	Mandatory Record
12.f	PRECEDENCE RECORDS	Mandatory for Precedence Method
12.g	UNIT COST RECORD(S)	Optional for Unit Cost Projects
12.h	PROGRESS RECORD(S)	Mandatory for Updates
12.i	FILE END RECORD	Last Record of Data File

12. Record Descriptions:

a. Volume Record:

The Volume Record shall be used to control the transfer of data that may not fit on a single disk. The first record in every disk used to store the data exchange file shall contain the Volume Record. The Volume Record shall sequentially identify the number of the data transfer disk(s). The Volume Record shall have the following format:

Description	Column Position	Max. Len.	Reqd. Value	Type	Just.
RECORD IDENTIFIER	1— 4	4	VOLM	Fixed	Filled
DISK NUMBER	6— 7	2	—	Number	Right

(1) The RECORD IDENTIFIER is the first four characters of this record. The required value for this field shall be "VOLM."

(2) The DISK NUMBER field shall identify the number of the data disk used to store the data exchange information. If all data may be contained on a single disk, this field shall contain the value of "1". If more disks are required, then the second disk shall contain the value "2", the third disk shall be designated with a "3", and so on. Identification of the last data disk shall not be accomplished with the Volume Record. Identification of the last data disk is accomplished in the PROJECT END RECORD (see Paragraph 12.i).

b. Project Record:

The Project Identifier Record is the first record of the file and shall contain project information in the following format:

Description	Column Position	Max. Len.	Reqd. Value	Type	Just.
RECORD IDENTIFIER	1— 4	4	PROJ	Fixed	Filled
DATA DATE	6— 12	7	—	ddmmmyy	See (2)
PROJECT IDENTIFIER	14— 17	4	—	Alpha.	Left
PROJECT NAME	19— 66	48	—	Alpha.	Left
CONTRACTOR NAME	68—103	36	—	Alpha.	Left
ARROW OR PRECEDENCE	105	1	A,P	Fixed	
CONTRACT NUMBER	107—112	6	—	Alpha.	Left
PROJECT START	114—120	7	—	ddmmmyy	Filled
PROJECT END	122—128	7	—	ddmmmyy	Filled

(1) The RECORD IDENTIFIER is the first four characters of this record. The required value for this field shall be "PROJ". This record shall contain the general project information and indicates which scheduling method shall be used.

(2) The DATA DATE is the date of the schedule calculation. The abbreviation "ddmmmyy" refers to a date format that shall translate a date into two numbers for the day, three letters for the month, and two numbers for the year. For example, March 1, 1999 shall be translated into 01Mar99. This same convention for date formats shall be used throughout the entire data format. To insure that dates are translated consistently, the following abbreviations shall be used for the three character month code:

Abbreviation	Month
JAN	January
FEB	February
MAR	March
APR	April
MAY	May
JUN	June
JUL	July
AUG	August
SEP	September
OCT	October
NOV	November
DEC	December

(3) The PROJECT IDENTIFIER is a maximum of four character abbreviation for the schedule. These four characters shall be used to uniquely identify the project and specific update as agreed upon by Contractor and Contracting Officer. When utilizing scheduling software these four characters shall be used to select the project. Software manufacturer's shall verify that data importing programs do not automatically overwrite other schedules with the same PROJECT IDENTIFIER.

(4) The PROJECT NAME field shall contain the name and location of the project edited to fit the space provided. The data appearing here shall appear on scheduling software reports. The abbreviation "Alpha.", used throughout Paragraph Six, RECORD DESCRIPTIONS, refers to an "Alphanumeric" field value.

(5) The CONTRACTOR NAME field shall contain the Construction Contractor's name edited to fit the space provided.

(6) The ARROW OR PRECEDENCE field shall indicate which method shall be used for calculation of the schedule. The value "A" shall signify the Arrow Diagramming Technique. The value "P" shall signify the Precedence Diagramming Technique. The ACTIVITY IDENTIFICATION field of the Activity Record shall be interpreted differently depending on the value of this field (see Paragraph 12.e.2). The Precedence Record shall be required if the value of this field is "P" (see Paragraph 12.f).

(7) The CONTRACT NUMBER field shall directly identify the contract for the project. For example, a complete government construction contract number, "DACA85-89-C-0001", shall be entered into this field as "890001".

(8) The PROJECT START shall contain the date that the project will start or has started. On government construction projects, this date is the date that the construction contractor acknowledges the Notice to Proceed.

(9) The PROJECT END shall contain the data that the contract must complete on or prior to. On government construction projects, this date is the PROJECT START plus the contract period, which is typically expressed in a specific number of calendar days.

c. Calendar Record:

The Calendar Record(s) shall follow the Project Identifier Record in every data file. A minimum of one Calendar Record shall be required for all data exchange activity files. The format for the Calendar Record shall be as follows:

Description	Column Position	Max. Len.	Reqd. Value	Type	Just.
RECORD IDENTIFIER	1— 4	4	CLDR	Fixed	Filled
CALENDAR CODE	6— 6	1	—	Alpha.	Filled
WORKDAYS	8—14	7	SMTWTFS	See (3)	
CALENDAR DESCRIPTION	16—45	30	—	Alpha.	Left

(1) The RECORD IDENTIFIER shall always begin with "CLDR" to identify it as a Calendar Record. Each Calendar Record used shall have this identification in the first four columns.

(2) The CALENDAR CODE shall be used in the activity records to signify that this calendar is associated with the activity.

(3) The WORKDAYS field shall contain the work-week pattern selected with "Y", for Yes, and "N", for No. The first character shall be Sunday and the last character Saturday. An example of a typical five (5) day work-week would be, NYYYYYN. A seven (7) day work-week would be, YYYYYYY.

(4) The CALENDAR DESCRIPTION shall be used to briefly explain the calendar used.

d. Holiday Record:

Optional Holiday Record(s) shall follow the Calendar Record(s). The Holiday Record shall be used to designate specific non-work days for a specific Calendar. More than one Holiday Record may be used for a particular calendar. If used, the following format shall be followed:

Description	Column Position	Max. Len.	Reqd. Value	Type	Just.
RECORD IDENTIFIER	1— 4	4	HOLI	Fixed	Filled
CALENDAR CODE	6— 6	1	—	Alpha.	Filled
HOLIDAY DATE	8— 14	7	—	ddmmmyy	Filled
HOLIDAY DATE	16— 22	7	—	ddmmmyy	Filled
HOLIDAY DATE	24— 30	7	—	ddmmmyy	Filled
HOLIDAY DATE	32— 38	7	—	ddmmmyy	Filled
HOLIDAY DATE	40— 46	7	—	ddmmmyy	Filled
HOLIDAY DATE	48— 54	7	—	ddmmmyy	Filled
HOLIDAY DATE	56— 62	7	—	ddmmmyy	Filled
HOLIDAY DATE	64— 70	7	—	ddmmmyy	Filled
HOLIDAY DATE	72— 78	7	—	ddmmmyy	Filled
HOlIDAY DATE	80— 86	7	—	ddmmmyy	Filled
HOLIDAY DATE	88— 94	7	—	ddmmmyy	Filled
HOLIDAY DATE	96—112	7	—	ddmmmyy	Filled
HOLIDAY DATE	114—120	7	—	ddmmmyy	Filled
HOLIDAY DATE	122—128	7	—	ddmmmyy	Filled

(1) The RECORD IDENTIFIER shall always begin with "HOLI" and shall signify an Optional Holiday Calendar is to be used.

(2) The CALENDAR CODE indicates which work-week calendar the holidays shall be applied to. More than one HOLI record may be used for a given CALENDAR CODE.

(3) The HOLIDAY DATE is to be used for each date to be designated as a non-work day.

e. Activity Records:

Activity Records shall follow any Holiday Record(s). If there are no Holiday Record(s), then the Activity Records shall follow the Calendar Record(s). There shall be one Activity Record for every activity in the network. Each activity shall have one record in the following format:

Description	Column Position	Max. Len.	Reqd. Value	Type	Just.
RECORD IDENTIFIER	1— 4	4	ACTV	Fixed	Filled
ACTIVITY IDENTIFICATION	6— 15	10	—	See (2)	
ACTIVITY DESCRIPTION	17— 46	30	—	Alpha.	Left
ACTIVITY DURATION	48— 50	3	—	Integer	Right
ACTIVITY COST	52— 60	9	—	Integer	Right
CONSTRAINT DATE	62— 68	7	—	ddmmmyy	Filled
CONSTRAINT TYPE	70— 71	2	—	See (7)	
CALENDAR CODE	73— 73	1	—	Alpha.	Filled
HAMMOCK CODE	75— 75	1	Y,blank	Fixed	

(continued)

Description	Column Position	Max. Len.	Reqd. Value	Type	Just.
WORKERS PER DAY	77— 79	3	—	Integer	Right
RESPONSIBILITY CODE	81— 84	4	—	Alpha.	Left
WORK AREA CODE	86— 89	4	—	Alpha.	Left
MOD OR CLAIM NUMBER	91— 94	4	—	Alpha.	Left
BID ITEM	96— 99	4	—	Alpha.	Left
UPI CODE	101—105	5	—	See (15)	
USER DEFINED 1	107—110	4	—	See (16)	
USER DEFINED 2	112—115	4	—	See (16)	
USER DEFINED 3	117—120	4	—	See (16)	
USER DEFINED 4	122—125	4	—	See (16)	
USER DEFINED 5	127—130	4	—	See (16)	

(1) The RECORD IDENTIFIER for each activity description record must begin with the four character "ACTV" code. This field shall be used for both the Arrow Diagram Method (ADM) and Precedence Diagram Method (PDM) (see Paragraph 12.b.6).

(2) The ACTIVITY IDENTIFICATION consists of coding that shall differ, depending on whether the ADM or PDM method was selected in the Project Record (see Paragraph 12.b.6). If the ADM method was selected, then the field shall be interpreted as two right-justified fields of five (5) integers each. If the PDM method was selected, the field shall be interpreted as one (1) right-justified field of ten (10) integers each. The maximum activity number allowed under this arrangement is 99999 for ADM and 9999999999 for the PDM method.

(3) The ACTIVITY DESCRIPTION shall be a maximum of 30 characters. Descriptions must be limited to the space provided.

(4) The ACTIVITY DURATION contains the estimated duration for the activity on the schedule. The duration shall be based upon the work-week designated by the activity's related calendar (referenced in 12.e.8).

(5) The ACTIVITY COST contains the estimated earned value of the work to be accomplished in the activity.

(6) The CONSTRAINT DATE field shall be used to identify a date that the scheduling system may use to modify float calculations. If there is a date in this field, then there must be a valid entry in the CONSTRAINT TYPE field. The CONSTRAINT DATE shall be the same as, or later than, the PROJECT START DATE. The CONSTRAINT DATE shall be the same as, or earlier than, the PROJECT END DATE.

(7) The CONSTRAINT TYPE field shall be used to identify the way that the scheduling system shall use the CONSTRAINT DATE to modify schedule float calculations. If there is a value in this field, then there must be a valid

entry in the CONSTRAINT DATE field. Below are the minimum list of entries for the CONSTRAINT TYPE. Other types of constraints may be available from specific software manufacturers.

Code   Definition

ES   The CONSTRAINT DATE shall replace an activity's early start date, if the early start date is prior to the CONSTRAINT DATE.

LF   The CONSTRAINT DATE shall replace an activity's late finish date, if the late finish date is after the CONSTRAINT DATE.

(8) The CALENDAR CODE, as previously explained, relates this activity to an appropriate work-week calendar. The ACTIVITY DURATION must be based on the valid work-week referenced by this CALENDAR CODE field (see Paragraph 12.e.4).

(9) The HAMMOCK CODE indicates that a particular activity does not have its own independent duration, but takes its start dates from the start date of the preceding activity (or node) and takes its finish dates from the finish dates of its succeeding activity (or node). If the value of the HAMMOCK ACTIVITY field is "Y", then the activity is a HAMMOCK ACTIVITY.

(10) The WORKERS PER DAY is an *optional* field that shall contain the average number of workers expected to work on the activity each day the activity is in progress. The total duration times the average number of workers per day shall equal the Contractor's estimate of the total man-days of work required to perform the activity.

(11) The RESPONSIBILITY CODE shall identify the Subcontractor or major trade involved with completing the work for the activity.

(12) The WORK AREA CODE shall identify the location of the activity within the project.

(13) The MOD OR CLAIM NUMBER code is an *optional* field that shall uniquely identify activities that are changed on a construction contract modification, or activities that justify any claimed time extensions.

(14) The BID ITEM is an *optional* field that shall designate the bid item number associated with the activity.

(15) The Construction Specification Institute Masterformat CSI CODE is an *optional* field and not required to meet the data exchange standard. The CSI CODE shall contain the value of code corresponding to the work to be accomplished in this activity.

(16) USER DEFINED fields are *optional* fields. They are provided to allow for a fixed expansion of capabilities for individual very large projects that may require additional fields.

f. Precedence Record:

The Precedence Record(s) shall follow the Activity Records if a Precedence type schedule (PDM) is identified in the ARROW OR PRECEDENCE field of the Project Record (see Paragraph 12.b.6). the Precedence Record has the following format:

Description	Column Position	Max. Len.	Reqd. Value	Type	Just.
RECORD IDENTIFIER	1 — 4	4	PRED	Fixed	Filled
ACTIVITY IDENTIFICATION	6 — 15	10	—	Integer	See (2)
PRECEDING ACTIVITY	17 — 26	10	—	Integer	
PREDECESSOR TYPE	28 — 29	2	—	See (4)	
LAG DURATION	31 — 34	4	—	Integer	Right

(1) The RECORD IDENTIFIER shall begin with the four character "PRED" in the first four columns of the record.

(2) The ACTIVITY IDENTIFICATION identifies the activity whose predecessor shall be specified in this record. Refer to the Activity Record for further explanation on this field (see Paragraph 12.e.2).

(3) The PREDECESSOR ACTIVITY number is the number of an activity that precedes the activity noted in the ACTIVITY IDENTIFICATION field.

(4) The PREDECESSOR TYPE field indicates the type of relation that exists between the chosen pair of activities. The PREDECESSOR TYPE field must, as a minimum, contain one of the codes listed below. Other types of activity relations may be supported from specific software vendors.

Code	Definition
SS	Start-to-Start relation
FF	Finish-to-Finish relation
FS	Finish-to-Start relation (conventional)

(5) The LAG DURATION field contains the number of days delay between the preceding and current activity.

g. Unit Cost Record:

The Unit Cost Record shall follow all Precedence Records. If the schedule utilizes the Arrow Diagram Method, then the Unit Cost Record shall follow any Activity Records. The fields for this record shall take the following format:

Description	Column Position	Max. Len.	Reqd. Value	Type	Just.
RECORD IDENTIFIER	1 — 4	4	UNIT	Fixed	Filled
ACTIVITY IDENTIFICATION	6 — 15	10	—	Integer	See (2)
TOTAL QTY	17 — 27	11	—	Floating	Pt.
COST PER UNIT	29 — 39	11	—	Floating	Pt.
QTY TO DATE	41 — 51	11	—	Floating	Pt.
UNIT OF MEASURE	53 – 55	3	—	Alpha.	

(1) The RECORD IDENTIFIER shall be identified with the four character "UNIT" placed in the first four columns of the record.

(2) The ACTIVITY IDENTIFICATION for each activity shall match the format described in the activity record (see Paragraph 12.e.2).

(3) The TOTAL QTY is the total amount of this type of material to be used in this activity. This number consists of eight digits, one decimal point, and two more digits. An example of a number in this format is "11111111.11". If decimal places are not needed, this field shall still contain a ".00" in columns 25, 26, and 27.

(4) The COST PER UNIT is the cost, in dollars and cents, for each unit to be used in this activity. This number consists of eight digits, one decimal point, and two more digits. An example of a number in this format is "11111111.11". If decimal places are not needed, this field shall still contain a ".00" in columns 37, 38, and 39.

(5) The QTY TO DATE is the quantity of material installed in this activity up to the data date. This number consists of eight digits, one decimal point, and two more digits. An example of a number in this format is "11111111.11". If decimal places are not needed, this field shall still contain a ".00" in columns 49, 50, and 51.

(6) The UNIT OF MEASURE is an abbreviation that may be used to describe the units being measured for this activity.

h. Progress Record:

Progress Record(s) shall follow all Unit Cost Record(s). If there are no Unit Cost Record(s), then the Progress Record(s) shall follow all Precedence Records. If the schedule utilizes the Arrow Diagram Method, then the Progress Record shall follow any Activity Records. One Record shall exist for each activity in-progress or completed. The fields for this Record shall take the following format:

Description	Column Position	Max. Len.	Reqd. Value	Type	Just.
RECORD IDENTIFIER	1— 4	4	PROG	Fixed	Filled
ACTIVITY IDENTIFICATION	6—15	10	—	Integer	See (2)
ACTUAL START DATE	17—23	7	—	ddmmmyy	Full
ACTUAL FINISH DATE	25—31	7	—	ddmmmyy	Full
REMAINING DURATION	33—35	3	—	Integer	Right
COST TO DATE	37—45	9	—	Integer	Right

(1) The RECORD IDENTIFIER shall begin with the four character "PROG" in the first four columns of the record.

(2) The ACTIVITY IDENTIFICATION for each activity for which progress has been posted, shall match the format described in the Activity Record (see Paragraph 12.e.2).

(3) An ACTUAL START DATE is required for all in-progress activities.

The ACTUAL START DATE shall be the same as, or later than, the PROJECT START date contained in the Project Record (see Paragraph 12.b.8). The ACTUAL START DATE shall also be the same as, or prior to, the DATA DATE contained in the Project Record (see Paragraph 12.b.2).

(4) An ACTUAL FINISH DATE is required for all completed activities. If the REMAINING DURATION of an activity is zero, then there must be an ACTUAL FINISH DATE. The ACTUAL FINISH DATE must be the same as, or later than the PROJECT START date contained in the Project Record (see Paragraph 12.b.8). The ACTUAL FINISH DATE must also be the same as, as or prior, to the DATA DATE contained in the Project Record (see paragraph 12.b.2).

(5) A REMAINING DURATION is required for all in-progress activities. Activities completed, based on time, shall have a zero (0) REMAINING DURATION.

(6) Cost progress is contained in the field COST TO DATE. If there is an ACTUAL START DATE, then there must also be some value for COST TO DATE. The COST TO DATE is not tied to REMAINING DURATION. For example, if the REMAINING DURATION is "0", the COST TO DATE may only be 95% of the ACTIVITY COST. This difference may be used to reflect 5% retainage for punch list items.

i. File End Record:

The File End Record shall be used to identify that the data file is completed. This record shall be the last record of the entire data file. The File End Record shall have the following format:

Description	Column Position	Max. Len.	Reqd. Value	Type	Just.
RECORD IDENTIFIER	1 — 3	3	END	Fixed	Filled

(1) The RECORD IDENTIFIER for the File End Record shall be "END". No data contained in the data exchange file that occurs after this record is found shall be used.

Appendix B

Good Scheduling Practices[1]

I. GENERATING SCHEDULES

A. General Conditions

1. The construction schedule must begin on the Notice to Proceed date (NTP), and complete on or before the contract completion date.
2. Activity identification numbers should only be integers.
3. Ranges of activity identification numbers should be chosen to reflect physical areas of construction.
4. Activity descriptions should utilize a standard set of abbreviations or words.
5. Standardized coding schemes (Construction Specification Index (CSI), Building Specification Index (BSI), TYPE, RESP, etc.) should be used, if not conflicting with coding requirements in contract specifications.

B. Defining Appropriate Activities

1. Contract-specific milestones must be included in the network.
2. Specific activities should be included for any permits that are required.
3. Activity classifications should include submittal, approval, procurement, delivery, installation, test, inspection, etc.
4. All submittal and procurement activities not specifically included in the progress schedule should be kept in another system that can automatically check approval and delivery dates with submittal activities.
5. Subcontractor submittal activities should be specifically identified.
6. Installation activity levels of detail should reflect differences in trade productivity (e.g., studs, drywall, taping).

---

[1]Excerpted from: De La Garza-Rodriguez, Jesus M. *A Knowledge Engineering Approach to the Analysis and Evaluation of Schedules for Mid-Rise Construction.* Construction Engineering Research Laboratory Technical Report P-90/70 March 1990, Champaign, IL.

7. Installation activity levels of detail should reflect differences in splitting activities due to weather sensitivity (e.g., drywall and taping).
8. Installation activities should be split into physical locations, rather than percentages complete.

Activity Durations

9. If subcontract activities have durations longer than 20 days, that subcontractor must provide a fully integrated subnetwork.
10. Approval activities for contractor-certified items will, generally, be two weeks in duration.
11. Approval activities for architect-engineer approval will, generally, be one month in duration.
12. Long-duration procurement is appropriate for new technology or remote sites. However, all procurement activities over 60 days in duration should be reviewed.
13. Installation activities should, generally, range between 5 and 25 days.

Activity Logic

14. The general progression of activities should be submit, approve, procure, deliver, install, and test.
15. Steel structures should, generally, be represented by the following series of activities: submit steel, approve steel, procure steel, deliver steel, erect steel, install metal deck, install deck slab, and fireproof steel.
16. Cast-in-place structures should, generally, be represented by the following series of activities: submit concrete certification, submit rebar certification, submit concrete placement plan, approve concrete submittal, procure concrete materials, rebar delivery, install concrete forms, install rebar, install concrete, cure concrete, strip concrete forms, and move concrete forms.
17. Precast structure should, generally, be represented by the following series of activities: submit precast drawings, approve precast drawings, fabrication precast, deliver precast, install precast panels, install precast tie strips, install caulking, and seal precast.
18. The installation of partitions should be represented by the following series of activities: submit drywall partition system, approve drywall system, procure drywall system, deliver drywall system, install metal studs, install drywall, install drywall taping.
19. Mechanical rooms should be scheduled as early as possible to give access to the installation crews.

20. Exterior closure should incorporate separate activities for the building "skin" and window installation.
21. In some cases, sealing and caulking the exterior after window installation should be included.
22. In high- and midrise buildings, the building skin of the first and second floors should, generally, be scheduled last.
23. In high- and midrise buildings, installation activities should, generally, be the same on every floor.

Critical Path

24. All activities that have a float of one working week or less should be considered critical activities.
25. If more than three parallel critical paths exist, it is likely that some durations have been overstated.
26. The ratio of critical to total activities should be reasonable. (A high ratio of critical to total activities suggests that the float has been manipulated, a low ratio of critical to total activities suggests that there is too little detail on critical path activities.)

Float

27. All activities with over 100 days of float should be investigated.
28. Installation activities with over 100 days of float are not properly integrated into the schedule.

Costs

29. No cost will be allowed on submittal or approval activities.
30. The cost of all activities may not exceed the contract amount.
31. Activity costs should range is between 0.1 and 2.5 percent of the total contract amount.
32. Unit prices and quantities of early activities should be the same as the prices and quantities of the same type of activity that occur later in the project, and activities that have larger quantities.
33. The ratio of the critical path cost to the total project cost should fall within an appropriate range.
34. Projects should not be front-end loaded.
    a. At 33 percent complete in time, the contractor should have received 25 percent of the contract amount.
    b. At 66 percent complete in time, the contractor should have received 75 percent of the contract amount.

35. Delivery of electrical and mechanical activities may distort front-end analysis and should be reviewed.

II. IN-PROGRESS ANALYSIS

1. Analysis of current progress should monitor paths to which lagging activities belong.
   a. Variance between original dates and actual dates should be used to indicate schedule slippage.
   b. If there is a schedule slippage, the entire path to which the lagging activities belong should be marked for monitoring.
   c. Is it one delay or a combination of delays?
   d. Base the analysis on the number of activities, whose status is in progress or finished, that are already behind, as opposed to those projected to be behind.
   e. Material procurement delays may be identified as a one-time occurrence, several delays with the same type of material, or a delay with all procurement leading up to a specific activity.
   f. Subcontractor delays may be identified by identifying the performance factors by subcontract codes.
   g. Weather delays may be identified as delays of similar activities along several paths through the schedule during discrete periods of time.
   h. Productivity delays may be assessed by determining the projected man-hours per day to man-hours spent each day.
2. Analysis of current progress should be based on contractor's past performance.
   a. The rate of float consumption should be identified.
   b. The rate of duration used per period should be identified.
   c. Determine whether the delay is likely to continue. If it is, then apply these rates to similar activities that use the same crew or subcontractor.
   d. Activities do not need to be revised based on positive rates of consumption.
   e. Activity durations should be adjusted based on the negative rates of productivity.
   f. The ratio of days to make up to total days remaining should be less than 0.2.
3. Method of determination as to how to recover lost time.
   a. Analyze activities with remaining durations greater than 20 days to see whether durations may be shortened.
   b. Determine whether sequential critical activities can be performed concurrently.

   c. Perform cost/time trade-off analyses.

   d. Attempt to accelerate prime contractor work before evaluating sub-contract work.

4. Activities of similar types should show consistent productivity rates.

5. Analyses of change orders should be reasonable.

   a. Float has more value early in the project, due to the potential of unknown delays.

   b. Float has more value, the smaller the quantity that is available to be placed. Larger quantities are less sensitive to small changes.

   c. All directly impacted activities should be coded to indicate the claim number and modification to which the activity belongs.

   d. Compare the currently approved plan to the plan generated after the changes to the network have been processed.

   e. Quantify schedule impact in terms of activities directly impacted and those indirectly impacted.

Appendix C

Software Products Illustrated in This Book

Primavera Project Planner, Version 3.2
  Primavera Systems, Inc.
  Two Bala Plaza
  Bala Cynwyd, PA 19004

PlanTRAC 4B
  Computerline, Inc.
  P. O. Box 1100
  Auburn, MA 01501

ViewPoint, Version 3.1
  Computer Aided Management, Inc.
  1318 Redwood Way
  Suite 210
  Petaluma, CA 94954

Open Plan, Version 3.2
  Welcom Software Technology
  15995 N. Barkers Landing
  Suite 275
  Houston, TX 77079

PMS-II, Version 9.0
  North America Mica, Inc.
  11772 Sorrento Valley Road, #134
  San Diego, CA 92121

PMS80 Project Management Software, Version 6.00
  Pinnell Engineering, Inc.
  5441 S.W. Macadam Avenue, Suite 208
  Portland, OR 97201

PROMIS, Version 3.0
  Strategic Software Planning Corp.
  150 Cambridge Park Drive
  Cambridge, MA 02140

Aldergraf Scheduling System, Version 4.2/3
  Aldergraf Systems, Inc.
  1080 W. Sam Houston Parkway North
  Suite 113
  Houston, TX 77043

PPMS-30000, Version 3.6
  Advanced Project Analysts
  8432 Sterling #201
  Irving, TX 75063

Index